Contract Pastoral Care and Education: The Trend of the Future?

Contract Pastoral Care and Education: The Trend of the Future? has been co-published simultaneously as *Journal of Health Care Chaplaincy,* Volume 9, Numbers 1/2 1999.

Contract Pastoral Care and Education: The Trend of the Future?

Larry VandeCreek, DMin
Editor

Contract Pastoral Care and Education: The Trend of the Future? has been co-published simultaneously as *Journal of Health Care Chaplaincy,* Volume 9, Numbers 1/2 1999.

Routledge
Taylor & Francis Group
New York London

First Published by

The Haworth Pastoral Press, 10 Alice Street, Binghamton, NY 13904-1580 USA

The Haworth Pastoral Press is an imprint of The Haworth Press, Inc., 10 Alice Street, Binghamton, NY 13904-1580 USA.

This edition published 2012 by Routledge

Routledge
Taylor & Francis Group
711 Third Avenue
New York, NY 10017

Routledge
Taylor & Francis Group
2 Park Square, Milton Park
Abingdon, Oxon OX14 4RN

Contract Pastoral Care and Education: The Trend of the Future? has been co-published simultaneously as *Journal of Health Care Chaplaincy*, Volume 9, Numbers 1/2 1999.

Cover design by Thomas J. Mayshock Jr.

Library of Congress Cataloging-in-Publication Data

Contract pastoral care and education: the trend of the future? / Larry VandeCreek, editor.
p. cm.
Includes bibliographical references and index.
ISBN 0-7890-0793-2 (alk. paper) – ISBN 0-7890-0826-2 (alk. paper)
1. Pastoral counseling centers. 2. Chaplains, Hospital. 3. Contracting out. I. VandeCreek, Larry.
BV4012.25 .C66 1999
253–dc21

99-051929

Contract Pastoral Care and Education: The Trend of the Future?

CONTENTS

ABOUT THE EDITOR

Larry VandeCreek, DMin, BCC, is Director of Pastoral Research at The HealthCare Chaplaincy in New York City. For the past 23 years, he held faculty and staff positions with The Ohio State University College of Medicine and Public Health and its associated medical center. Dr. VandeCreek is a member of numerous professional associations including the American Association of Marriage and Family Counselors, the Association of Professional Chaplains, Inc., the American Association of Pastoral Counselors, and the Association for Clinical and Pastoral Education. He has published many journal articles which examine aspects of the relationship between religious faith and illness. Dr. VandeCreek is the author of *A Research Primer for Pastoral Care and Counseling* (Journal of Pastoral Care Publications, 1988) and is Co-Editor of *The Chaplain-Physician Relationship* (1991). He is Editor of the *Journal of Health Care Chaplaincy* (The Haworth Press, Inc.) which has published *Ministry of Hospital Chaplains: Patient Satisfaction* (1997), and *Scientific and Pastoral Perspectives on Intercessory Prayer: An Exchange Between Larry Dossey, M.D. and Health Care Chaplains* (1998).

Introduction

Larry VandeCreek, DMin, BCC

Chaplains need to tell their story! It is the story of how religious and spiritual ministries within health care are helpful.

The story must be told to various audiences. It needs to be told to a wide array of health care professionals and administrators as well as to health maintenance executives and health care consulting companies. We also need to tell some aspects of the story to ourselves.

This latter audience is the focus of this volume–to hold up a largely unexplored facet of our own story concerning chaplains who develop free-standing pastoral care and education organizations. They incorporate themselves and contract their services to health care organizations.

Now is the time to tell this story. Institutional pastoral care and education are heavily dependent upon the structure of the health care system and that system is changing in ways that often are not very friendly. Many departments are being reduced in size and chaplains have lost their jobs. In some centers (perhaps many), concern and pessimism concerning the future of institutional ministry are the order of the day.

From one perspective, this pessimism emerged after assumed invincibility was shattered. There was an era in many pastoral care and education programs in which cautionary words about the possibility of more stringent limitations were met with disdainful smiles. To such pastoral care department directors and staff chaplains, the wave after wave of financial curtailments came as a severe narcissistic blow. Fear, desperation, and depression followed.

Some chaplains (perhaps many) have become creative. Necessity is, as the

[Haworth indexing entry note]: "Introduction." VandeCreek, Larry. Published in *Contract Pastoral Care and Education: The Trend of the Future?* (ed: Larry VandeCreek) The Haworth Pastoral Press, an imprint of The Haworth Press, Inc., 1999, pp. 1-3. Single or multiple copies of this article are available for a fee from The Haworth Document Delivery Service [1-800-342-9678, 9:00 a.m. - 5:00 p.m. (EST). E-mail address: getinfo@haworthpressinc.com].

old maxim states, the mother of invention. They are finding ways to fight their way through the chaos of change. Somewhere between assumed invincibility and abject depression lies the energy to be creative.

One expression of this creativity and change within institutional pastoral care and education is the increasing number of freestanding centers. As far as this editor can determine, no one has collected and published their stories. A brief survey of the pastoral literature revealed only one publication that gave attention to contract pastoral care and education. In 1982, the College of Chaplains (now the Association of Professional Chaplains) produced a tape in their Care Cassette Library titled "Contracting Pastoral Services" (Vol. 9; #4). In it, Drs. Ronald Ropp, John Florell, and Clyde Getman described the Illinois Pastoral Services Institute of Bloomington, Illinois. They discussed theological foundations for contracting ministry services to other organizations, marketing strategies, and the delivery of services. The first purpose of this volume is to tell the history and stories of nine such centers. Hopefully they are representative of this phenomonon in the field of pastoral care and education.

And what do we think about freestanding centers? The second purpose of this volume is to raise that question. It has not been widely discussed in print either. Perhaps some think that there is little to discuss, but others likely disagree. Given all the changes in the health care system, are chaplains professionally and economically safer when working for a freestanding center? Given all those health care changes that cut back positions, will professional pastoral care have to increasingly rely on such freestanding centers as the only way into health care institutions? And what about Contract Pastoral Education (CPE) programs in freestanding centers? Some of them have created unique program structures. For example, must a supervisor be physically present at the site, an employee of the organization? These are questions of substance and five chaplains respond. They are involved in the field in a wide variety of ways. Some have never held national office; some have held such positions in the past while others are current leaders. This volume will serve its purpose if it generates interest, discussion and informed decision-making concerning the future of institutional pastoral care in the era of health care reform.

The third purpose of this collection is to provide information to others who are exploring the feasibility of or planning to establish a freestanding center. I asked authors to include some "how to . . . " suggestions. Their responses provide a wealth of experience and models as to how freestanding centers can be created.

I am sure that additional freestanding pastoral care and education organizations exist beyond those represented here. It was impossible to be comprehensive. I simply included those centers that came to my attention as I planned this volume. Even so, I have had to accommodate their contributions to the necessary page limits of the publication. To avoid any hint of preference, I have arranged their stories in alphabetical order according to the name of the organization. Responses are ordered according to the respondent's name.

THE STORIES OF NINE FREESTANDING CENTERS

The Ecumenical Institute, Cherokee, Iowa

Gene Sitzmann, MSW

SUMMARY OF MISSION

The mission of the Ecumenical Institute is to provide quality pastoral education through an accredited training center by certified personnel on an ecumenical, non-discriminatory basis in compliance with all local, state, and federal laws and to provide these services primarily on behalf of the people of Northwest Iowa. Special concern is directed to meeting the needs of rural communities and to serving as a public trust in all matters related to the financial support of these educational services.

HISTORY

The CPE program began at the Cherokee Mental Health Institute (CMHI) in 1967 when ACPE Supervisor/Chaplain Robert C. Alexander joined the

Father Gene Sitzmann is Chaplain-Educator, The Ecumenical Institute, 1251 West Cedar Loop, Cherokee, IA 51012 (E-mail: gsitzma@dhs.state.ia.us).

[Haworth co-indexing entry note]: "The Ecumenical Institute, Cherokee, Iowa." Sitzmann, Gene. Co-published simultaneously in *Journal of Health Care Chaplaincy* (The Haworth Pastoral Press, an imprint of The Haworth Press, Inc.) Vol. 9, No. 1/2, 1999, pp. 5-11; and: *Contract Pastoral Care and Education: The Trend of the Future?* (ed: Larry VandeCreek) The Haworth Pastoral Press, an imprint of The Haworth Press, Inc., 1999, pp. 5-11. Single or multiple copies of this article are available for a fee from The Haworth Document Delivery Service [1-800-342-9678, 9:00 a.m. - 5:00 p.m. (EST). E-mail address: getinfo@haworthpress inc.com].

staff. Cherokee possessed an attractive reputation as an active, progressive treatment center and teaching hospital with a patient census of 450 and an AMA Accredited Residency in Psychiatry. At the peak of the state hospital "warehousing" era, its census reached 1,729 patients (1945). In that era many lived out their lives at the "Insane Asylum" and approximately 829 were buried in a cemetery on the grounds, totally abandoned by their families and communities.

Starting in the early 1950s, progressive administrators and psychoactive medications led to the "de-warehousing" era and by 1977 the census stood at 238 patients. The new active treatment model was allowing more patients to return to their homes.

I joined the staff as a Chaplain-Intern in 1972. Following that year of training under Chaplain Alexander, I continued in pastoral education training and was certified as a CPE Supervisor with the National Association of Catholic Chaplains in 1974. In 1976, I completed a University of Iowa Masters degree in Social Work and have co-supervised CPE programs with Chaplain Alexander since then. Although "retiring" in 1986, Chaplain Alexander has continued his services on a part-time, volunteer basis to this date. Our years together were synergetic because of training we received and then applied to pastoral education, e.g., Gestalt, Transactional Analysis, Latent Language, Symbolism/Myth, and especially, Family Systems.

So, why envision a change in focus and funding? Because, just as anticipated in the planning that first began ten years ago, our daily census now averages just 75 inpatients!

The factors influencing this downsizing were:

- decreasing rural population,
- increasing community-based care services,
- an effective "new generation" of medications,
- an intensive treatment focus, e.g., Managed Care and the expectations and limitations set by both public and private pay resources, and
- higher standards and requirements for psychiatric training centers resulting in the loss of our accredited AMA program.

Mostly, we have been right on track with anticipating the impact of the developments in health care delivery that have occurred during this time and have adjusted both the Mission of the Ecumenical Institute and the timing of its fulfillment accordingly. Our goal has been to develop an alternative source of funding in order to finance the pastoral education needs of the new millennium for this rural area. Programs, as they are developed, will be distinct from those traditionally offered on the CMHI campus. Still, all such community-based activities–in churches, community colleges, hospitals, etc.–are being planned to operate complementarily with the current on-campus CPE programs. We anticipate continued State funding of my position until my retirement a few years from now.

For all of three decades now, our CPE program has remained unchanged in format, consisting of a full-time summer unit and an extended Fall-Spring unit. The summer unit has gathered seminarians and those in other institutional settings that held them fully occupied the other months of the year. The extended unit has typically gathered clergy and non-ordained persons within driving distance (often up to 100 miles or more) who sought entry-level or continuing education. As a result of continuity and the consistency of this programming, the center has developed a cadre of support parishes, institutions and alumni throughout this area who can now be called upon to lend support to the Mission of the Ecumenical Institute.

Fundamentally, we see ourselves by history as well as by current mission as an organization that can serve the pastoral education needs of rural congregations and their geographic communities. Congregations (like all rural school districts) are facing the need to merge–to "cluster"–and to cooperate in order to survive. Often this results in the loss of direct pastoral care services. The enrollment in recent years suggests that many laypersons wish to offer pastoral assistance but they have not been able to claim a pastoral identity. This is available to them primarily through the training and support provided by CPE. The extended units offered at this time serve the unique needs of this group and do so more adequately when the supervisor does the traveling and thereby provides CPE where "the living human document" lives. A pilot program offered recently in the community of Sheldon, Iowa was enormously successful and students continued in proximity to each other for continuing support, ecumenical interaction and pastoral care development at the community level. This is why we are convinced that the community, when more fully advised, engaged and appropriately challenged, will financially support the Mission of this Institute.

We have come a long way since the organizational meeting of the Institute in November 1993. The Board of Directors is now well informed, dedicated and effectively moving to fulfill the Mission. Our funding goal is to establish an endowment of some two million dollars. This would be developed through a baseline of participation, county by county, of $100,000 total in gifts and pledges from the residents of a given county. Planning to serve a network of the 24 counties of Northwest Iowa sets the ultimate goal of full community-based participation at $2,400,000. At this time, we have the first member of the network in place (Sioux County) through a family gift of $100,000. This, together with other assets accrued, builds the Institute's total capital to $160,000. It is calculated that a $2 million (plus) endowment fund would generate enough annual income to run a community-based program largely as it has operated at CMHI, i.e., two supervisors, salary and benefits as well as an adequate budget for other program costs. When the fund's assets have reached $500,000 guaranteeing adequate finances for at least five to seven years, the first supervisor will be hired to commence the "Outreach" program. Currently we hope to initiate this program by the year 2000. Board members have already made long-range commitments that will add a significant amount to the Institute's assets through life insurance beneficiary and other estate plans that members have or are establishing to benefit the endowment. Fund development would continue until a second supervisor could be hired. Both supervisors would be "itinerants" for the area, programming according to the interest and need of student participants. At a later time, after being well-established in the community and probably 10 to 20 years into the new millennium, additional fund-raising would allow possible expansion of programs if needed.

THE BOARD OF DIRECTORS

- They were recruited for diversity of religious affiliation, economic strata, gender, geographic residence, consumer representation and professional/personal background.
- They were recruited with the above in mind through personal contacts, interviews and engagements. A high priority was given to involving both "clinical" and "pastoral" representatives.
- Members are active through regular meetings (quarterly) on-site and by serving as the "Professional Consultation Committee" that meets regularly with students for both initial and exit interviews.
- At this point the Board serves in a "transitional" capacity, learning what will be needed to take over the management of both the ongoing funding and the day-to-day operation of an accredited, effective and creative community-based pastoral education program. When adequately funded, the Board will assume the full management of the CPE Program. The current host institution will continue to be a supportive but non-funding institution, thereby bringing to full effect a gradual transition and ultimately a reversal of the roles between the State of Iowa and the Ecumenical Institute.

THE INTERFAITH COMMUNITY

Cued by the goal of providing community services on an ecumenical basis, the name of the organization was chosen to reflect that "ecumenism." The board represents the major religious denominations of NW Iowa: Lutheran (ELCA and LCMS), United Methodist, Roman Catholic, Presbyterian, and Reformed Churches. We have encountered no difficulties with this ecumenical approach and received many benefits, especially in broadening the base of interest and support.

FUNDING

We started with a "piggy bank" amount that has grown to major significance:

- A portion of student tuition ($25) was placed in a Development Account.
- Gifts/pledges of several thousand dollars were made by the two chaplain-supervisors.
- Board members began to give gifts and make pledges.
- We established Support Outreach Services (S.O.S.). Club Memberships (gift categories) are:
  Charthouse Club $250,000 and up
  Beacon Club $100,000-$249,999
  Rescuers Club $10,000-$99,999
  Signal Corps Club $1,000-$9,999
  Lamplighters Club $100-$999
  Sparks Club $0-$99.
- A major gift was received from a consumer board member and his extended family totaling $100,000 in land transfer value and in cash.
- Through mailings to all 825 attorneys of NW Iowa, each was advised of the mission of the Institute and each provided with a complete file for reference in serving their clients as estate and planned-giving agents. As a result, additional gifts and bequests are now being received from individuals in various other counties.

The Board has invested most of the cash assets in highly rated mutual funds that have increased handsomely during the Wall Street Bull Market. The only expenditures at this time are related to the fund-raising phase now under way so that the program can begin by the new millennium.

GOVERNMENTAL AGENCIES

The keys here are: communication-patience, communication-time, communication-assurance giving. Governmental agencies are directly responsible to the citizenry and as such are appropriately circumspect, cautious and conservative. We have fully and successfully committed the Mission of the Institute to the use of these three 'key' combinations by:

- securing the interest and support of the executive officers of the institution (CMHI) and the state officers in Des Moines,
- obtaining an incorporated status with the State of Iowa as a not-for-profit organization and an IRS (501c) tax exempt status, and by
- selecting and engaging board members who are persons of high visibility and public trust.

There is no possibility for either public or private support without these assurances being in place and actively cultivated.

THE PRODUCT

The "product" is stated in the Mission Statement noted above. The "consumers" are persons who seek to learn basic pastoral care skills or to enhance their current level of pastoral functioning.

INTERNAL STRUCTURE

The internal structure of the Institute at this time consists of:

- a constitution and by-laws (incorporation requirements),
- diversified board members who serve without compensation,
- officers and membership with specified terms and functions, and
- regular meetings with agendas directed to the fulfillment of the Mission Statement.

At this time, no one (including the supervisor) is compensated nor derives any benefit from organizational funds. When funding is adequate, the Board will hire employees (supervisors and support staff) and establish their compensation and benefit packages. Five years from now the transition should be complete. The Ecumenical Institute will have hired the staff to initiate, creatively organize and effectively operate a community-based and community-funded clinical pastoral education program designed to serve the needs of the rural communities of Northwest Iowa. Any needed expansion of the program will be achieved by establishing an Office of Development that will conduct Annual Appeals and develop an attractive format for Planned Giving.

GENERAL ADVICE (DO'S AND DON'TS)

Do

- Believe in your "product." For us, this constitutes our belief in effective pastoral care.

- Be patient.
- Dream "what might be" (my colleague calls this "think *wild*!").
- For assurance sake, be detailed, thorough and concise, yet visionary.
- Believe that people care about their caregivers and will support their pastoral formation and growth.
- Elect and engage diversity.
- Remember: "Rome wasn't built in a day"; still, "*Carpe diem!*"
- Demonstrate optimism because "Attitude is Everything."

Don't

- Lose heart nor forget the goal; it will keep you–and the mission–going.
- Succumb to nay-sayers, the faint-hearted or lackluster.
- Forget to thank and express appreciation for each and *every* word or action of support.
- Forget to "write home"; keep in touch with the community through timely and informational media coverage.

* * *

The logo chosen for The Ecumenical Institute is the Lighthouse.

"Together let us BRIGHTEN the lamp in the Lighthouse of Pastoral Care"

The Foundation for Interfaith Research and Ministry, Houston, Texas

Ronald H. Sunderland, EdD

MISSION STATEMENT

The Foundation for Interfaith Research and Ministry (FIRM) promotes, sponsors, and conducts interfaith and interdisciplinary programs of scholarship, research, education, and service.

HISTORY

In 1985, a few clergy began to respond to the growing Houston AIDS population. It consisted of two strands. Dr. Earl Shelp, then a faculty member of the Institute of Religion's program in Medical Ethics co-sponsored by Baylor College of Medicine and Rice University, employed Jay, a Rice University student in philosophy as a graduate assistant. Jay's periodic bouts of ill health led to medical tests and diagnostic procedures disclosed he was HIV+. This realization and his care as his condition deteriorated brought the needs of people with HIV disease sharply to our attention. The second strand was interwoven with Jay's history as Dr. Ron Sunderland pursued his task of determining how the chaplaincy service at the M. D. Anderson Cancer and

---

Ronald H. Sunderland is Vice President, The Foundation for Interfaith Research and Ministry, 701 North Post Oak Road, Suite 330, Houston, TX 77024 (E-mail: firm-hou@neosoft.com) (Web page: www.neosoft.com/~firm-hou).

[Haworth co-indexing entry note]: "The Foundation for Interfaith Research and Ministry, Houston, Texas." Sunderland, Ronald H. Co-published simultaneously in *Journal of Health Care Chaplaincy* (The Haworth Pastoral Press, an imprint of The Haworth Press, Inc.) Vol. 9, No. 1/2, 1999, pp. 13-27; and: *Contract Pastoral Care and Education: The Trend of the Future?* (ed: Larry VandeCreek) The Haworth Pastoral Press, an imprint of The Haworth Press, Inc., 1999, pp. 13-27. Single or multiple copies of this article are available for a fee from The Haworth Document Delivery Service [1-800-342-9678, 9:00 a.m. - 5:00 p.m. (EST). E-mail address: getinfo@haworthpressinc.com].

Tumor Institute could adapt procedures designed for bed-side pastoral ministry to the hospital's growing number of outpatients. By 1984, the number of outpatient visits had surged to over 2,000 per day. Chaplaincy services, effective as they were at the bedside, had not been translated into effective responses in the clinics. The first national OutPatient Ministry Conference, held at M. D. Anderson in 1984, identified many of the barriers to outpatient pastoral care but few answers.

Perhaps the most important conference conclusion was the realization that chaplaincy services in hospitals and other clinical settings tended to operate on the assumption that chaplains were the primary pastoral care providers to inpatients. We realized that this certainly was not true for outpatients who spent a few hours each week in the institutional setting. For outpatients who were members of local congregations, their communities of faith carried primary responsibility for pastoral care. The conference report called for a partnership that linked family, congregation, and hospital as a caring network. In particular, hospital chaplains and pastors of families were thought of as partners who needed to look to one another for support so that they could better serve the families to whom they were committed.

As part of the effort to determine effective pastoral strategies, Sunderland, also a faculty member at the Institute of Religion, was assigned to an outpatient chemotherapy clinic. In 1984, he began to meet the first AIDS patients who were receiving chemotherapy in the unit. As Sunderland and Shelp began to extend their ministry beyond the hospital to the homes and apartments of people with AIDS, the desperate needs of these first AIDS patients became clear. They were meeting these patients weeks, sometimes days, prior to their deaths as their status rapidly deteriorated. One day Shelp noticed a patient sitting in the clinic waiting area hours after his appointment with the physician and clinic staff was completed. He was waiting for a friend to drive him to his apartment, but had no idea when his friend would come. Shelp drove his car to the hospital, picked up the patient, and drove him home. Realizing the man's greatest fear was of dying alone in his apartment, Shelp decided to spend the night, assuring him that he would not be abandoned. By the end of the second week, one clergy friend after another had been conscripted to sit with this dying patient overnight, and one was with him as he died.

Similar relationships developed as a few laypersons joined this group of clergy; with increasing experience, the team became known as the 'Mary Magdalene Mission Squad.' As the outlines of the new epidemic became clearer, additional strands were added to the cord that bound the team together. Shelp and Sunderland wrote the first article calling the church's attention to the needs of these patients; "AIDS and the Church" was published by *The Christian Century* in September 1985. The first clergy press conference in the nation was convened at Houston's South Main Baptist Church in January 1988. The first clergy workshop to acquaint community priests, pastors, and rabbis with the growing epidemic was held in the same church, also in January, 1986; over 150 clergy listened to presentations by epidemiologists, physicians, social workers, city health department staff, and clergy.

The clergy group, now known as the "Clergy Consultation on AIDS," realized that the one-on-one care provided by the buddy program would be overwhelmed by the sheer scope of patients' needs for bedside care, transportation, meals, and support of companions and family members as their loved ones died. As congregations, hesitantly at first, indicated their interest in the Consultation's efforts, groups of laypeople–"Care Teams"–were formed. Consisting of 12 or more persons, Care Team members were assigned in sub-groups ('mini-teams') of 5-7 members per AIDS client family. A team of 24 members cared for up to 4 families. By the end of 1986, six Care Teams were functioning, and that number doubled by December 1987. What had begun as a spontaneous, ad hoc response to the first wave of HIV-infected people had taken on a life of its own. In 1988, the Associated Catholic Charities of New Orleans asked Shelp and Sunderland to help them write a proposal to the Robert Wood Johnson Foundation based on the Houston Care Team program. We proposed that the program encompass New Mexico, Oklahoma, Texas, Arkansas, and Louisiana, using CPE centers as training and supervision facilities. Sunderland introduced the program in Arkansas, and Shelp in Oklahoma; the care team program was already well established in Texas. The grant was based on the use of clinical training and supervision as proposed but the Associated Catholic Charities did not pursue the cooperation with the ACPE centers. Consequently, many local sites lacked effective oversight.

THE MOVE FROM HOSPITAL TO HOME CARE

This primary focus on in-home care for individuals with special needs was less revolutionary than it might appear. First, only one Houston hospital was providing inpatient care. Most AIDS-related care was outpatient. Second, hospitals were already reducing hospital stays in the effort to restrain rising costs. Surgeries that previously required a seven-to-fourteen day stay were being performed in 'day hospitals.' Third, once a patient's immediate health crisis was addressed, care became outpatient focused, particularly with respect to chemotherapy and radiotherapy administration. Fourth, Sunderland had worked with the lay pastoral ministry concept since 1973 and was convinced that the local congregation was the proper location for pastoral ministry. He believed that laypersons, if trained and clinically supervised, were equipped to provide effective pastoral services. Fifth, the Care Team model from the beginning was founded in the church's rich theology that links three biblical strands. Each of these is now described.

THEOLOGICAL FOUNDATIONS FOR THE PASTORAL MINISTRY OF CONGREGATIONAL MEMBERS

Pastoral ministry as a congregational activity incorporates three inter-related theological strands: (1) baptism and its obligations; (2) the gifts or "charisms" of the Holy Spirit and consequences of the Spirit's presence in baptized individuals' lives; and (3) the New Testament concept of interdependence–"Bear one another's burdens, and so fulfill the law of Christ" (Gal. 6:2). Each of these strands consists of many threads which, when bound together, contribute to the strength of the cord that binds congregations together in loving and compassionate care. Each is now briefly discussed.

Baptism

Baptism and its meaning provide the theological basis for congregations and members to engage in pastoral care. In baptism, Christians are lodged within the community of faith, identified with the death and resurrection of Christ, are marked with the presence of the Holy Spirit in their lives, and are called, or ordained, to ministry. Incorporation into the community of faith places one under care and nurture. Christian theology interprets Ezekiel's prophecy (36:25-26) as announcing baptism: "I will sprinkle clean water upon you, and you shall be clean from all your uncleanness, . . . A new heart will I give you, and a new spirit I will put within you (gift of the Holy Spirit); . . . (I will) cause you to walk in my statutes and be careful to keep my ordinances (life in faith), and you shall be my people and I will be your God" (becoming part of the Church). Baptism signifies, as a sharing in the paschal mystery, a confession of sins and change of heart as recipients are pardoned, cleansed, justified, and sanctified by Christ, in the power of the Holy Spirit.[1] The consequence is the obligation to follow Christ, that is, to manifest in the believer's life the attributes of life in Christ (Matt. 16:24; Mk. 8:34, 10:21; Luke 9:23, 18:22; Jn. 10:27, 12:26). Baptism is defined clearly by Paul (I Cor. 12:13 and Gal. 3:27-28) as setting a person within the Body of Christ: "God sets a man within, not merely informs him that he is set within, the Body of Christ."[2] We are made one in Christ as we are engrafted into the community of God's people, the Church.

In his statement that "the ministry of the church is exercised by every man, woman, and child who bears the mark of baptism,"[3] James Fenhagen underscores the importance of the relationship between baptism and the believer's call to ministry. Fenhagen amplified his conviction in a subsequent book, stating he believed deeply that laypeople are called by virtue of their baptism to share in the ministry of the Gospel, even suggesting that the term 'layperson' should be abolished altogether in reference to the ministry of the church, "in order that we might emphasize the interdependence inherent in our baptism. . . . To speak of total ministry in the church is to speak of a ministry of all the baptized, each dependent on the gifts of the other."[4] That is, baptism and ministry are inextricably linked; ministry is an obligation, not an option; baptism is the ordination to ministry for every member of the household of faith.

The Gift of the Holy Spirit and the Gifts of the Spirit

The Holy Spirit is present in the believer's life as Comforter (Jn. 14: 16, 26). The Spirit is the unifying power by which Christians are made one in Christ and equipped to live the life of faith. With the indwelling of the Holy Spirit, Christians are gifted for ministry. Adopted as children of God at baptism, Christians receive the gift of the Holy Spirit, are born to the new life and made members of the church, the body of Christ, and restored to a place in the covenant with God (2 Cor. 1:21-22; Eph. 1:13-14). The task of the Spirit is to bind Christians into community that expresses the Spirit of Christ Jesus in their communion with one another. This mighty task is complete only when members build each other up in a love which is expressed, for example, in the Parable of the Last Judgment (Matt. 25: 31-46).

The presence of the Spirit is accompanied by bestowal of *charisms*–gifts of ministry. Paul is at pains to point out that all do not have identical gifts (e.g., Romans 12:4-8 and I Cor. 12:4-13: see also Eph. 4:7-18). Christians are to employ the gifts each has been given in the service of Christ, "from whom the whole body, joined and knit together by every joint with which it is supplied, when each part is working properly, makes bodily growth and builds up itself in love" (Eph. 4:16). The gifts for ministry are many and varied because that is what the body requires in order to be fully operational; their purpose is fulfilled when all the gifts are coordinated and used for the whole body. For this reason, one gift supersedes others, namely the gift of love, because it builds up the body. "Love is not jealous, conceited, or proud, but rejoices equally in the gifts of others" (I Cor. 13). Bernard Cooke[5] proposes that we are faced with both the possibility and the need to pay "renewed respect" to the action of the Holy Spirit in the community, particularly to the Spirit's charismatic designation of Christians for special ministerial roles. Further, he reminds us that since the discernment of spirits is something that involves the whole church, the entire community must participate in the discovery of the gifts (charisms) granted to individuals or groups for the sake of the church.

Mutual Responsibility and Interdependence in the Body of Christ

By the end of the first century, the Christian community had clearly established what Cooke calls "the gospel ideal of shepherding service" (pp. 350-351) based on the images of Jesus as Servant and Shepherd. Victor Furnish concurs, suggesting that the greatest contribution Paul made to the church was his impressive demonstration of how the gospel and the Christian ministry are fundamentally and absolutely inseparable. "Paul saw that 'the truth of the gospel' (Gal. 2:14) must manifest itself concretely in the life of the Christian community and in the individual lives of Christian believers wherever they are in the world."[5] Furnish adds that, like Jesus, Paul established a pastoral model that he expected his congregations to follow (I Cor. 12:26; II Cor. 11:29; Gal. 8:2, 10). Paul's pastoral ministry and missionary activity was rooted in the character and meaning of the Gospel which to him implied that members of the community were to "bear (share) one another's burdens, and so fulfill the law of Christ" (Gal. 6:2). According to Furnish, Paul's nurture of the congregations he established is an overlooked aspect of the apostle's ministry. Even today, this nurture includes "strengthening the fabric of the Christian community, giving guidance and support to its members as they confront perplexing moral choices, providing leadership as the church formulates its responses to pressing social issues, comforting the sick and the bereaved, and giving counsel and aid to those in any kind of need."[6] Paul understood that these shepherding, nurturing ministries occupy a central place:

> That one's service to Christ involves serving others is brought out clearly in the discussion of Romans 14 about the "strong" and the "weak" in the congregation. Each member of the community should "walk in love" toward every other member (Rom. 14:15). When one "thus serves Christ," Paul concludes, "one is acceptable to God and approved by men" (v. 18). Diakonia, then, is one of the signs of life in the body of Christ, and when it ceases to be a vital force, both Christian community and the praise of God likewise fail.[7]

NATIONAL REPLICATION OF THE CARE TEAM CONCEPT

FIRM was incorporated in September 1988, when it was clear that the Care Team program had reached a stage of development that required more than the part-time attention of Shelp and Sunderland. During this same time period, Shelp and Sunderland published the first volumes concerning the church's ministry to those with AIDS. These included: *AIDS: Personal Stories in Pastoral Perspective; AIDS and the Church*; *AIDS: A Manual for Pastoral Care; Handle With Care: A Manual for Congregations Caring for*

People with AIDS; and *AIDS and the Church: The Second Decade* (see publication information at the end of this chapter). By 1992 over 60 congregations in the greater Houston area were assigned at any one time to more than 220 individuals and families affected by AIDS. The total number of hours of Care Team ministry exceeded 670,000 by 1998. From its small beginnings in the mid-1980s, the AIDS Care Team model had been replicated by single congregations and interfaith networks in more than 75 cities in at least 30 states, many on the basis of presentations by Shelp and Sunderland, or using their books as a guide.

The innovative concept of Care Team ministry developed by Shelp and Sunderland has achieved national recognition. In 1992, Shelp received an America's Award from the Norman Vincent Peale Positive Thinking Foundation. Sunderland was the recipient of the 1997 Rosalynn Carter Caregiving Award for his leadership in the development of lay pastoral education. FIRM was one of 18 organizations selected from 3,500 nominations to receive the 1998 President's Service Award at a White House ceremony. The award is sponsored jointly by The Points of Light Foundation and the Corporation for National Service.

APPLICATION OF THE CARE TEAM MODEL TO OTHER DISEASES

The Care Team concept was adapted in 1992 to address the needs of Houston's caregivers involved with Alzheimer's and other dementia diseases. By mid-1998, nearly 25 Alzheimer's Care Teams were assigned to at least 125 Alzheimer's care partners (the term is used in preference to 'clients' and as a means of emphasizing the partnership that links Care Team members with the individuals and families they serve). In 1994, the model was expanded yet again to provide in-home, hands-on support to frail elderly, and then to frail adults generally. Their needs, similar to the first two disease groups, are so intense and so extensive that the customary one-on-one model of congregational pastoral care is immediately overwhelmed. Care Teams in this segment of FIRM's ministries are termed "Second Family Care Teams" because they function as 'second families' to these persons. At the time of writing, FIRM is in partnership with 80 Houston-area congregations that have developed AIDS, Alzheimer's, and Second Family Care Teams. Over 1,300 Care Team members are involved weekly in the care of families that will number over 600 in 1998. Since 1994, Sunderland and Shelp have assisted agencies in eight cities in Minnesota, Ohio, South Carolina, Texas, Washington, and Wisconsin to introduce Second Family programs to congregations in their respective communities.

THE TRAINING AND SUPERVISION OF CARE TEAMS

FIRM's staff provides three essential services to the Care Teams and their congregations. First, the foundation provides the stable administrative base from which effective, healthy teams operate. While each team is a ministry of and accountable to its congregation, FIRM personnel serve as adjunct staff members to the congregations, releasing clergy from the day-to-day management tasks. Second, FIRM assists each new congregation in the recruitment of its Care Team, orients and trains them, and provides on-site supervision by participating in their monthly Care Team meetings. Third, FIRM provides continuing education conferences and workshops so that team members can hone and upgrade their pastoral skills. The system, with its emphasis on intensive oversight of Care Team members, is an application of the clinical pastoral education model.

MINISTRY IN A MULTI-CULTURAL SETTING

From its outset in 1985, FIRM's ministry was multi-cultural. African American and Spanish-speaking laypersons served with whites in many teams. However, the majority of Care Team members were from predominantly white congregations although Brentwood Baptist church, an Afro-American congregation, remains the largest AIDS Care Team with over 60 members. We remember vividly the black AIDS client who looked into Shelp's eyes and thanked him for his care, but added, "I wish that just once I would look up and see a black hand holding mine." In 1997-98, FIRM engaged Hispanic and Afro-American staff members in order to facilitate the adaptation of the Care Team model to those congregations. We recognized that although there were a number of large African American congregations involved, minority congregations would be recruited more effectively from within their own cultures. More important, although we had demonstrated that care was given effectively without regard to color or cultural background (e.g., blacks ministered to whites, Jews to Catholics, Baptists to Catholics), we doubted that our white staff members could access minority groups with the facility demonstrated by these two new staff members. The growth of the Care Team model in Hispanic congregations is of special interest because Spanish-speaking people will become the majority ethnic group in the 'sun-belt' states early in the new millennium. Our efforts are a small contribution to more effective pastoral education for Spanish-speaking pastors and lay members.

FIRM'S EDUCATION AND RESEARCH COMMITMENT

FIRM is committed to education and research; it demonstrates this by the journal articles and books produced by its staff. Sunderland and Shelp have authored over 60 journal articles and initiated research in partnership with the University of Texas School of Public Health to examine the incidence of burnout and unresolved grief in AIDS Care Team members. They are presently under contract with Abingdon Press for a book that will provide a theological and biblical foundation for Care Team ministry. *Ministries of Sustaining Presence* will be published in 1999. In addition to its focus on the extension and support of congregational Care Teams, FIRM has a commitment to other aspects of congregational education. Sunderland is continuing the development of his "Equipping Lay People for Ministry" program that trains persons for the congregation's basic pastoral ministry to members and is the basis for the focus on supervision of lay pastoral ministers. Second, Sunderland's work in grief education attracted a two-year grant to FIRM by the Open Society Institute's "Project on Death in America" funded by financier George Soros. The two-year project is assisting ten congregations to develop coordinated grief education and support programs. This pilot project is now being enlarged to incorporate the training of school counselors and teachers so that they can be responsive to student grief. Plans are under way to develop a curriculum that could be introduced into school curriculums.

BOARD OF TRUSTEES

A Board of Trustees governs FIRM and represents a broad cross section of Houston's business community. FIRM's administrative staff and Board members share the fund-raising tasks. Grant writing is the province of the staff, while general income development draws on the skills and business contacts of Board members. Board members are presently engaged in a study of a proposed long-range developmental plan that includes capital fund promotion. FIRM's most successful fund-raising project, providing 25-30 percent of the annual budget, is its "Sweet Charity" gala held on the Sunday nearest Valentine's Day. The dinner benefits from long-term partnerships with Houston's premier chefs, and annually honors individuals who have played a significant part in founding and maintaining FIRM's programs. Training and supervisory activities are provided to partner congregations without fee, a parallel to the care of individuals outside the congregation's membership who receive services at no fee. Approximately 15 percent of congregations include FIRM in their outreach budgets, and this number grows annually. In 1994, FIRM entered into a partnership with the Houston/Harris County Area Agency on Aging, which in 1998 provided 10 percent of FIRM's budget in recognition for support of a growing number of frail, low income elderly. The Board created The Acorn Foundation as a FIRM subsidiary to serve as an endowment fund. One of its purposes is to provide financial security for FIRM staff, most of whom are funded by soft money grants. FIRM can draw on reserves to buffer staff against the loss of a significant grant and to provide a 'breathing space' when and if major changes occur in FIRM's funding cycle. In the absence of major problems, funds will accrue against future downturns.

FIRM has benefited from its status as a freestanding interfaith organization, but its present fiscal and organizational stability has been hard won. In 1988, Shelp and Sunderland acted in faith that their vision was realizable and would attract the interest and commitment of funding agencies. That faith has been vindicated. FIRM was the first agency in Houston to receive state AIDS funding, followed subsequently by acquisition of federal Ryan White grants that preceded the rapid increase in minority-based AIDS programs after those funds began to flow. Corporate and private foundation support has provided a stable foundation on which to build other types of funding, particularly the Sweet Charity gala. Congregational support, approximately 10 percent of the annual budget, is not required of our partner congregations, but more congregations are including FIRM in their outreach budgets. The affirmation of Sunderland's grief-related program in the form of the Open Society Institute's "Project on Death in America" grant is indicative of the support that is possible once a program's basic integrity has been demonstrated to funding agencies.

STRUCTURE OF THE CORPORATION'S PROGRAMS

FIRM has functioned from its inception as an interfaith agency with Care Teams drawn from Jewish and Christian congregations. Conversations have been initiated with Houston's growing Islamic community to examine ways in which the Care Team concept might be adapted to Islamic family needs. Conversations will begin shortly with representatives of the various Asian communities. FIRM's activities are based on partnerships with local congregations and their supporting judicatories. Each Care Team is fully integrated into the pastoral ministry of its congregation, is an extension of the congregation's basic pastoral care of members, and is accountable to the congregation. Lay Care Team leaders selected from the team both coordinate the assignments of members to the team's care partners (clients) and keep the clergy informed of the team's activities.

Application of the Care Team model to two additional areas is in the developmental stage. Grief Care Teams are a logical next step, and one large Catholic parish (4000+ families) has in fact implemented this step. As we gain experience from this pilot effort, other Grief Care Teams will follow. Second, application of the concept to support families caring for chronically ill and catastrophically disabled children is even more urgent. Many of these families disintegrate in the face of the child's needs. The child's father often abandons the family, further endangering the child. FIRM has not yet identified adequate funding for this project, and other barriers have yet to be resolved, for example, the screening and stricter supervision of adults who work with children.

FIRM looks to the future with the strong conviction that its partnerships with local congregations have resulted in programs that meet needs of frail adults, needs that previously were not addressed. Individuals and member families with intense and extensive health care concerns can now receive congregation-based care and support that turns their night into day. The story is told best from the perspective of a family caregiver.

A CARE TEAM CASE STUDY

Mike and Helen, married 41 years and with two happily married sons, looked forward to retirement with more time to travel, especially to visit their grandchildren. Mike planned to teach his oldest grandson fly-fishing during the next school vacation. He sang in the choir of the congregation of which they were founding members. Helen was a member of the women's circle that met in members' homes. Mike had been concerned for some months that Helen had become forgetful, on one occasion dressing to attend the circle meeting that was not scheduled until the following week. A week later, she left to drive to her meeting, but never arrived. When a member phoned him to ask about Helen, he anxiously drove around the neighborhood until he found her sitting in her car, seemingly lost. A visit with their physician led to a series of tests and a diagnosis of possible Alzheimer's disease. The doctor suggested that Helen should not drive alone in the future.

Mike turned away offers from friends to pick her up on their way to meetings. He was embarrassed at the turn of events and he did not want them to see her confused state. His retirement plans were put on hold; it was weeks since he had even thought of playing his weekly game of golf. With Helen now requiring full-time oversight, he first resigned from the choir that had been one of his greatest sources of satisfaction and fulfillment and then from the men's Bible study group of which he was a founding member. His whole life now revolved around Helen's protection and comfort. He rejected offers of others to sit with her–he reminded his pastor that he had committed to love and honor her in sickness and in health, and he meant to keep that pledge.

Only with great reluctance did he agree, months later, to accept the assistance of the Care Team his pastor pressed on him. The team was composed of the members of Helen's former women's circle, who co-opted their husbands to invite Mike to join them at golf while they sat with Helen. The partnership between Mike and the Care Team members grew as Mike acknowledged their contribution had lifted a burden. The burden of Helen's deteriorating mental state they could not lift. But at least he could rejoin the choir, because two of the women met him in the narthex each Sunday before worship and sat with Helen. If she became restless, they quietly left the sanctuary and met Mike after the service. Soon, Care Team members were picking Helen up, driving to the nearby shopping center and 'walking the mall' with her. As stores opened, they would open the shopping list Mike had given them and assist Helen in the purchase of items with cash she drew from her purse. She enjoyed these outings, clearly relishing her shopping trips. Care Team members, now comfortable being with Helen in public, invited the couple to join a Tuesday brunch group. Mike is now fully re-socialized, surrounded by members of the congregation, enjoying the respite opportunities the team provides, and, importantly, persuaded by his pastor that his acceptance of Care Team support is a theological statement about what it means to be a member of the community of faith. When Helen dies, his grief will be shared by his Care Team members because they have also shared his grief over the long course of her illness.

A CARE TEAM NETWORK IN EVERY COMMUNITY

When Dr. C. Everett Koop visited the Houston Care Team program in 1988, he reviewed our work and stated: "I think that what you have done here is absolutely tremendous. You are way ahead of the rest of the country. If it would be possible to take what you have done to other parts of the country, we would see networks such as you have here spring up all over the land." Dr. Koop's vision is being realized. Returning to the theme addressed earlier, the FIRM Care Team program embodies the ideal of a network of care that, if available in every community, would guard against families 'dropping through the cracks.'

In the absence of such a program, intense and excessive family needs that are not susceptible to traditional one-on-one support are often overlooked. For example, when Alzheimer's Care teams were being promoted, we began with Houston's largest congregations, since they would have the greatest concentration of families with special needs and the largest reservoir of lay ministers who could serve them. If the data promulgated by the Alzheimer's Association and the U. S. Public Health Service are accurate, there are approximately 4 million Alzheimer's sufferers (one-seventieth of the population). In a congregation of 5,000 members, 70 families would be afflicted. Yet we were unable to identify any congregation that helped more than a small handful of these families prior to adopting the Care Team ministry. Only after our painstaking effort to identify and serve these families did we convince pastoral staffs to recognize the needs of these affected individuals and their families. This lack of care is highly correlated with the low level of clergy awareness concerning the needs of dementia-stricken families.

The replication of the Care Team model in the states listed above was achieved by the readiness of church-related institutions to become resources to their communities. They acquired the Care Team model as a new aspect of their community outreach, assigning staff to work with area congregations, training their lay members and providing oversight of their Care Teams. Institutional chaplains are ideally equipped to provide such services if hospitals and nursing homes/retirement centers are willing to make the necessary commitment to community outreach. With shortened hospital stays and families' needs for in-home support during convalescence, it seems an obvious strategy because it links hospital and congregation in the care of people with special needs. This should be of particular interest to hospital chaplains, whose ministry could thereby be more effectively integrated with congregational pastoral care of the families they both serve.

STAFFING

FIRM has seven full-time and one half-time staff members. Administratively, the burden of funding personnel, office expenses, travel to Care Team meetings, all of which occur in teams' congregational settings, is constant and heavy. We set out deliberately to offer the program to congregations at no fee, not only to encourage smaller congregations to adopt the program, but to assert our role as a servant agency of congregations. We have no magic tricks that provide short cuts to financing; individuals involved in establishing freestanding agencies should engage in long-term financial planning. We will be pleased to correspond with those who may wish to consult with us. It seems noteworthy that the eight centers that we have assisted in the development of Care Team programs have all been based in existing community agencies with strong staff and financial resources. Persons may obtain information about these efforts by writing to them at the following addresses:

Ms. Ann Warner, Lutheran Social Services of the Miami Valley, 8430 Inner Mission Way, Dayton, OH 45459-7400 (Phone: 937-843-0020).

The Rev. Nancy Dietsch, Lutheran Homes of South Carolina, P. O. Box 444, White Rock, SC 29177 (Phone: 803-732-8734).

Ms. Cindy Fisher, Care Team Ministry Coordinator, Oakwood Village, 8201 Mineral Point Road, Madison, WI 53705 (Phone: 808-231-3456).

The Rev. Joy Mortenson-Wiebe, Lutheran Homes of Oshkosh, 225 North Eagle Street, Oshkosh, WI 54901-4196 (Phone: 920-235-3454).

Ms. V. Schutte, Fox Valley Lutheran Homes, P. O. Box 2753, Appleton, WI 54913-2753 (Phone: 920-734-8711).

Ms. Debbie Beard, Care Team Coordinator, Windcrest Alzheimer's Care Center, 8050 Hospital Drive, Abilene, TX 79808 (Phone: 915-692-1533).

Ms. Janine Canady, South Texas Interfaith Council, 5403 Everhart, Suite 1108, Corpus Christi, TX 78411 (Phone: 512-814-8585).

Ms. Nancy Slind, Josephine Sunset Homes, 9901 272nd. Place, Stanwood, WA 98292 (Phone: 360-629-2128).

REFERENCES

1. Max Thurian and Geoffrey Wainright, (ed.). *Baptism and Eucharist*. Geneva: World Council of Churches Publications, 1983; pp. 3, 4.

2. Oscar Cullmann, *Baptism in New Testament* (London: SCM Press, 1950), p. 31.

3. James Fenhagen, *Mutual Ministry* (New York: Seabury Press, 1977), p. 21.

4. James Fenhagen, *Ministry as Solitude* (New York, Seabury Press, 1981), pp. 1-14.

5. Bernard Cooke, *Ministry to Word and Sacraments* (Philadelphia: Fortress Press, 1978), p. 198.

6. Victor Furnish, "Theology and Ministry in the Pauline Letters," *A Biblical Basis for Ministry*, Earl E. Shelp and Ronald H. Sunderland, eds., (Philadelphia: Westminster Press, 1981), p. 102.

7. Victor Furnish, "Theology and Ministry in the Pauline Letters," *A Biblical Basis for Ministry*, Earl E. Shelp and Ronald H. Sunderland, eds., (Philadelphia: Westminster Press, 1981), p. 102.

8. Furnish, p. 118-119.

9. Furnish, p. 132.

STAFF PUBLICATIONS

Ronald H. Sunderland. (1977, 1981, 1983, 1997). *Equipping Laypeople for Ministry* (Houston: ELM Inc.).

Earl E. Shelp and Ronald H. Sunderland, (eds). (1981). *A Biblical Basis for Ministry* (Philadelphia: Westminster Press).

Earl E. Shelp and Ronald H. Sunderland, eds.,
The Pastor as Prophet (1985)
The Pastor as Servant (1986)
The Pastor as Priest (1987)
The Pastor as Theologian (1988)
The Pastor as Teacher (1989)
The Pastor as Counselor (1991)

Earl E. Shelp, Ronald H. Sunderland, and Peter Mansell. (1988). *AIDS: Personal Stories in Pastoral Perspective* (New York: Pilgrim Press).

Ronald H. Sunderland and Earl E. Shelp. (1986). *A Manual for Pastoral Care* (Philadelphia: Westminster Press).

Ronald H. Sunderland and Earl E. Shelp. (1990). *Handle With Care: A Handbook for Care Teams Serving People with AIDS* (Nashville: Abingdon Press).

Earl E. Shelp and Ronald H. Sunderland. (1991). *AIDS and the Church* (Philadelphia: Westminster Press).
Earl E. Shelp and Ronald H. Sunderland. (1992). *AIDS and the Church: The Second Decade* (Louisville: Westminster/John Knox Press).
Ronald H. Sunderland. (1993). *Getting Through Grief: Caregiving by Congregations* (Nashville: Abingdon Press).
Earl E. Shelp and Ronald H. Sunderland. (under contract). *Ministries of Sustaining Presence* (Nashville: Abingdon Press).
[Dr. Shelp is the general editor of the *Theology and Medicine* series of 8 volumes published by Kluwer Publishing Co.]

The HealthCare Chaplaincy, Inc., New York, New York

George F. Handzo, MDiv
Walter J. Smith, SJ, PhD
John Twiname, MDiv
Carolyn Twiname, MPA
Will Maitland Weiss, MFA

SUMMARY OF MISSION

The HealthCare Chaplaincy is a not-for-profit center for health-related pastoral care, clinical education and research. With a professional staff of 24 chaplains and 11 CPE Supervisors, "The Chaplaincy," as it is called, has developed a multifaith, multi-institutional "Partnership Model" providing pastoral care leadership for a growing number of medical and health-related facilities (see the appendix for a current list). At the same time, these institutions constitute a campus for educating annually over 250 students representing 30 or more different denominations and faith groups.

In connection with its new, seven-floor center in the heart of Manhattan, it has recently begun specialized community outreach programs, including sponsorship of a Jewish Institute for Pastoral Care, seminars for local clergy,

---

Rev. George F. Handzo is Director, Pastoral Care & Education, Memorial Sloan-Kettering Cancer Center, New York, NY. Rev. Walter J. Smith, SJ, is President and Chief Executive Officer; Rev. John Twiname and Carolyn Twiname are Life Trustees; and Will Maitland Weiss was Director of Development and Communications, all at The HealthCare Chaplaincy, Inc., New York, NY.

Address correspondence to: Rev. John Twiname, 307 East 60th Street, New York, NY 10022-1505 (E-mail jtwiname@healthcarechaplaincy.org).

[Haworth co-indexing entry note]: "The HealthCare Chaplaincy, Inc., New York, New York." Handzo George F. et al. Co-published simultaneously in *Journal of Health Care Chaplaincy* (The Haworth Pastoral Press, an imprint of The Haworth Press, Inc.) Vol. 9, No. 1/2, 1999, pp. 29-42; and: *Contract Pastoral Care and Education: The Trend of the Future?* (ed: Larry VandeCreek) The Haworth Pastoral Press, an imprint of The Haworth Press, Inc., 1999, pp. 29-42. Single or multiple copies of this article are available for a fee from The Haworth Document Delivery Service [1-800-342-9678, 9:00 a.m. - 5:00 p.m. (EST). E-mail address: getinfo@haworthpressinc.com].

and bereavement as well as other support groups. In a 13-year period of growth, the budget has risen from less than $300,000 per year to over $4 million in 1998.

HISTORY

The Chaplaincy began in 1961 when several churches and three hospitals created The East Midtown Protestant Chaplaincy, supporting one full-time professional chaplain who paralleled the charitable service rendered by the Roman Catholic Archdiocese and the New York Board of Rabbis.

In 1971, the Rev. James Jeffries, a CPE Supervisor, was added as Executive Director and he began an education program by placing students in the four participating hospitals that contributed modestly toward the total program cost. The Chaplaincy struggled to find the necessary funds from the churches and the community until, in 1978, a merger was arranged with a century-old pastoral visitor service (The Bible and Fruit Mission). This marriage brought with it a $500,000 dowry and established a more solid financial foundation for the agency, renamed The Hospital Chaplaincy, Inc.

By 1981, The Chaplaincy employed five staff chaplains and two CPE Supervisors (including the executive director), provided a full-year residency program and coverage in four hospitals and a nursing home, with a resident assigned to a fifth hospital. However, with only modest support from the churches and the hospitals, it could not attract sufficient support to avoid an operating deficit.

Following a period without an executive director, The Chaplaincy recruited a husband-wife team, the Rev. John and Carolyn Twiname, as Co-Presidents in 1983. This shifted the emphasis to a full-time management and development effort, and began the transformation of the small Protestant agency. A rabbi CPE Supervisor was recruited as well as a rabbi chaplain and a Roman Catholic sister who were added to staff. At the same time, a rabbi/seminary professor and a priest from the Archdiocese were added to the Board. The new multifaith approach was validated as more students entered the program. In turn, hospitals began to establish departments of pastoral care and education, using The Chaplaincy staff for administrative support and professional supervision.

In 1991, following the completion of a strategic plan that provided for management succession, the Board created an executive vice president position and recruited a seminary dean/priest/psychologist, the Rev. Dr. Walter J. Smith, S.J. He became responsible for the education and clinical services as well as relationships with, by then, nine medical facility partners. Dr. Smith became President two years later and has since led The Chaplaincy into its own new facility as well as expanded its activities into new areas of service, education (both clinical and public) as well as research.

THE BOARD OF TRUSTEES

Because the originating sponsors were Protestant churches and three hospitals, it must have seemed natural for the incorporating board to recruit other trustees from these constituencies. It became evident, however, that clergy and medical leaders did not have the necessary range of gifts and skills, including development contacts, business planning, public relations, financial control and other expertise. Consequently, as time went on, more lay people, at first from church congregations, were asked to become trustees.

A "catch 22" existed, as it does for many non-profit organizations: trustees were needed to do operational work such as balance sheets and budgets, grant proposals and press releases. Recognizing that sources of larger amounts of money must be solicited by peers in the community, The Chaplaincy needed to recruit those people who had access to such sources, but were too busy to serve on a board so involved in operational details. The challenge was, and is, simultaneously to develop the operational capacity of the administrative staff and the leadership profile of the board.

The networking process that enables an organization to recruit good staff is relevant for recruiting good trustees. With trustee recruiting, however, there is a greater need to develop a compelling case that convinces them to join the board. This is the same case that is needed for raising money. Thus another version of the "catch 22"; an organization needs money to buy the management skills that give confidence to prospective trustees, and needs trustees to help get the money and to recruit other influential trustees that permits the procurement of competent staff. The process is like rock climbing, a persistent struggle upward from one foothold to the next higher one.

The Chaplaincy's new management team in 1983 concluded that, even though chaplaincy staffs were being cut back elsewhere, there was a growing public interest in, and therefore potential support for the spiritual component of health and healing. By 1984, the Board also concluded that The Chaplaincy would attract more support from the medical facilities and the community if it included staff and trustees from the major faith groups. This recruitment effort began with the addition of Jewish and Roman Catholic clergy, and later added representatives of Islam and other faith groups present in the New York area.

Prospective board members were found who saw opportunity for important pioneering work in pastoral care and inter-religious collaboration. The staff, to their credit, turned the work inside out, opening doors to what had been a very private and closed system of clinical education and pastoral care service. Additional persons now understood and participated with excitement in the spiritual dimensions of health care. Trustee prospects were invited to make rounds with chaplains and sit in on verbatim sessions with students. Even more radical in overcoming the usual religious hubris was the discovery that these lay people (actually leaders from other professions) could be trusted to make policy in a field about which, most would assume, they initially knew next to nothing.

Currently, trustees lead and serve on the following key committees: Strategic Planning; Pastoral Care and Education; Development; Capital Campaign Steering Committee; Marketing and Communications; Finance and Investment (including audit sub-committee); Personnel; and Nominating. There are also non-trustee members who serve on these committees (e.g., one representative from each medical facility on Pastoral Care and Education; hospital wage and salary administrators on Personnel). Ad hoc committees are often formed as well (e.g., for accreditation reviews).

THE PRODUCT

The Chaplaincy's product is the establishment, recruitment, and assignment of staff to pastoral care and education departments in health care facilities. It includes the continuing professional supervision of this staff. The primary results we seek are, first, high quality spiritual support to patients, families and health care staff and, second, excellent clinical education for students. Beyond these priority services, The Chaplaincy's staffs are involved in various committees and programs of their institutions. For example, the chaplains at one medical center organize a biennial conference on religion and cancer sponsored by the institution; they involve other Chaplaincy staff members as presenters.

While chaplains in each institution organize their own program for Pastoral Care Week, the total Chaplaincy staff shares ideas, and can economically produce special materials for use across institutions. While each CPE supervisor manages his/her own program, student groups can join together for didactics and special events, attracting educational resources unavailable for smaller groups.

Research and the dissemination of results, another part of the mission, is still in its early stages, but the partnership with so many institutions provides rich opportunities. Chaplain staff members at each partner institution receive the benefits of the research results through a variety of educational and organizational programs.

The Chaplaincy staff is encouraged to engage in public service to a wide variety of organizations including congregations and professional or civic organizations. Benefits accrue not only to the recipient organizations but also to the medical facilities and to The Chaplaincy through these relationships.

From its earliest days, The Chaplaincy's staff provided voluntary public services by training pastoral visitors in congregations as well as offering other public education programs. Recently The Chaplaincy employed a CPE supervisor as Director of Community Education and Outreach, the Rev. Denise Haines, who coordinates the provision of public education and special support services that include clergy seminars, bereavement groups and CPE for those who are engaged in pastoral work beyond the partner institutions.

Another outreach initiative is the appointment of a rabbi CPE Supervisor, Israel Kestenbaum, to lead the Jewish Institute for Pastoral Care within The Chaplaincy. Just as the Christian community has seen The Chaplaincy as a resource center, the Institute will assure that the Jewish community also receives these benefits. As The Chaplaincy's diversity continues to develop, other formerly underrepresented religious communities will likely be served in similar ways.

ORGANIZATIONAL STRUCTURE

The Partnership Model produces many benefits for all parties, exceeding those obtained from the usual employee model. Some were described or implied in the foregoing. The basic strength parallels the fundamental rationale of business organizations for "out-sourcing": an organization should not spend its energy and resources performing tasks that others can do better and for less cost (for example, The Chaplaincy, itself, uses a firm to handle the payroll). As one hospital administrator put it, "What do I know about supervising a priest?"

Considerable professional *hubris* continues in every community, reasoning that every function is its direct responsibility because no one else can care as much or do as well. Eventually, though, institutional administrators realize that in the Partnership Model they not only benefit from a highly qualified "employee," but also get a very committed back-up organization of community leaders and professionals who are dedicated to helping them upgrade and maintain the highest standards in health-related pastoral care.

The Chaplaincy offers a guarantee of quality, assuming the responsibility for professional supervision while the medical facility management provides day-to-day administrative supervision. The administrators appreciate not having to worry about the support functions. Similarly, their human resources departments are pleased that The Chaplaincy takes responsibility for the arcane details of clergy payrolls, housing allowances and other tax-related accounting, denominational or other pension plans and the keeping of personnel records.

Each institution forms an interdisciplinary Pastoral Care & Education Advisory Committee which reviews priorities for coverage, conducts exit interviews with students, advocates for the program among other departments, and otherwise provides support and guidance. A member of this committee is invited to be on The Chaplaincy's counterpart board committee.

The Chaplaincy is both partner and consultant; the medical facility is partner and client. When an institution contemplates a new pastoral care and education program, The Chaplaincy conducts a feasibility study resulting in a formal proposal as to how to set up and staff the program. The Chaplaincy is in a better position than a hospital to recruit staff candidates because it has developed contacts in the field. In staffing several institutions, they possess more flexibility to hire a qualified professional with special attributes (e.g., an orthodox rabbi, a Muslim imam, etc.) and divide the time among two or more institutions. In the end, it is the medical facility, however, which decides on the candidate to be hired by The Chaplaincy.

When institutions desire pastoral care students, The Chaplaincy, again, is in a better position to attract them, saving the medical facilities the trouble of advertising to seminaries and religious judicatories. Moreover, a better balancing of religious and ethnic background can be accomplished beginning with a larger group of applicants. The CPE supervisors function as an ad hoc admissions committee.

Chaplains who value maximum autonomy may prefer the traditional employee model because there is less accountability. However, the risk is "burnout." The Chaplaincy not only negotiates the annual budget with the client medical facility; it also provides structure and reasonable boundaries in defining the objectives and expected productivity of the chaplain.

The Chaplaincy gathers its chaplains, pastoral educators, and staff for their own grand rounds and monthly staff meetings. There are support groups facilitated by outside, contract professionals, peer review protocols, and weekly gatherings for prayer and lunch.

In the end, though, this dual accountability requires the recruitment of chaplains who work well in teams and are able to balance the multiple accountabilities involved in belonging to a religious denomination, one or more professional associations, and, in this case, a healthcare institution and a professional center. There are tensions, after all, when, for example, meetings at the hospital and at The Chaplaincy conflict. These are usually easily resolved by prior planning and with the understanding of the institution's administrators.

There are questions concerning fringe benefits that arise when a group of chaplains in existing institutions form a Partnership Model in the community: "If we are not strictly employees of the medical facility any more, then we won't enjoy the same benefits." While this has potential for creating problems, the reverse can also be true. Some hospitals, for example, will not designate the clergy housing allowance. Those chaplains have no alternatives unless they are part of an organization like The Chaplaincy that recognizes the legitimacy of such benefits.

Most of the benefits of a larger non-profit organization can be preserved in a smaller one like The Chaplaincy. In fact, the small one may afford the enlargement of some benefits such as flexible pre-tax spending accounts (e.g., for non-insured health care expenses or child care) and the larger pension contribution required by denominations when this would be impossible for the larger institution. It is all part of the negotiation with the institutions that are looking at the total cost-benefit of an alternative arrangement. The health care provider/partner simply pays its share of program cost to The Chaplaincy and a Chaplaincy staff person specializing in the rules governing professionals in this field handles the administrative details.

While the public identity of the chaplain staff sometimes poses a problem, as when one is listed as a speaker at a congregation, staff try to use both identities: "ABC is staff chaplain (or CPE supervisor) of the XYZ Medical Center and staff member of The HealthCare Chaplaincy." For their part, Chaplaincy staff members have a double sense of pride in belonging to a groundbreaking professional center as well as to a major health care system or institution. However, inasmuch as 90 percent of their time is spent in the medical facilities, there is a question of loyalties which, in the early days, was unquestionably directed inwardly to The Chaplaincy because the hospitals did not recognize them financially. As the medical facilities have come to see them as "staff" and underwritten their salaries, the sense of mutual obligation has changed to a more centrifugal force–especially since the institutions have the greater prestige. The fact that The Chaplaincy, however, actually issues the paycheck is the lever that keeps the accountability sense in balance.

THE MULTIFAITH DIMENSION

Changing from a Protestant orientation to a multifaith commitment was a pragmatic move. It was absolutely necessary if The Chaplaincy was to service major medical facilities in the New York area. Medical facilities needed to avoid any appearance of religious preference and the alternatives were no institutionally supported pastoral services at all or a thorough going multifaith approach. At the same time, this new approach helped trustee involvement because they became enthusiastic as they experienced the stimulation of the multifaith environment.

There is surely some theological work to be done before entering into a multifaith structure. For some Christians who feel the need to "carry the banner of Christ" in their chaplaincy work, the idea of revising their vision of the organization's identity, its prayer life and its vocabulary may seem like a betrayal. However, a vision of how the Christ Spirit works among all people may make a multifaith strategy feel like a superb witness for Christ, especially in the humility and active gracefulness required to make sure professionals of all faiths feel like full members.

Offering a medical system a multifaith program has proved to have many advantages. It mitigates their exposure in the business of choosing from among faith representatives in staffing their program. The "Partnership Model" also provides a layer of protection from a potentially protesting faith group when someone is hired or fired from the pastoral care department. But more impact is felt within a hospital staff when they view clergy or religious professionals working with them as a close-knit team in the enterprise of healing. They think, "This is the way religion is supposed to work among God's children." People are sick of the divisiveness caused by religious differences and it is in the "caring for the sick" that all religions have a common commandment around which multifaith teams can work with a spirit of collaboration and mutual respect.

Board members and staff find their exposure to spiritually authentic persons of other faiths an inspiring experience. Benefits of this include not only increased knowledge about these other faith traditions, but also more inclusive and respectful language that takes account of these traditions. This is often evident in meaningful changes that occur when persons from these various faith groups are together. For example, invocations at The Chaplaincy affairs must be sensitive in their language to the multifaith nature of the audience. When food is served, provision must be made for those on Halal or Kosher diets.

Even the minor changes, however, add up to a pervasive culture shift requiring constant vigilance. As noted above, it is easy for Christian staff to perceive these changes as requiring sacrifice only from them. The reality of this situation, and the feelings attached to it, need to be dealt with openly within the community or they will generate resentment and divisiveness. Part of the problem is that Christians, as members of the dominant culture, fail to understand how pervasive Christian language and symbols are in our culture. Christians also mistake acquiescence on the part of members of a minority culture for acceptance.

A symbol of The Chaplaincy's struggle to be a truly multifaith organization is in something currently called "Gathering." From its earliest days, The Chaplaincy staff had a tradition of worshipping together regularly. For years, the chaplains met daily for prayer and sometimes for holy communion, mostly taken from the Episcopal Book of Common Prayer. Communion largely vanished when Roman Catholics joined the staff. Daily worship became weekly when the staff became too spread out. When the staff gained its first

Jewish members, they had to confront how Christian the worship practices were. Not only the words of hymns, but the music itself had to be recognized as Christian. The staff finally had to give up the idea that this time together represented worship in any normal sense.

A major breakthrough came with the realization that having a leader who contributes content (readings, homily, etc.) was a central part of the problem. As the leader, it was easier to be more concerned with making sure that what one said was not offensive than with making sure that the content had some meaning. The format was changed and the time together was then called "Meeting" after the Quaker Meeting. The leader only declared the meeting to have begun and ended. Staff members were free to be together in silence or to offer prayers, readings or songs that were meaningful to them. The caveat was that everything was to be offered as one's own personal statement rather than as something others were to participate in. For example, when praying, one says, "*I* would like to pray today for . . . " rather that "Let *us* pray today for . . . " The title of the time together later came to be called "Gathering" which more aptly describes the occasion and avoids the other meanings of "Meeting."

The process of going from Episcopal worship to Gathering has been very helpful in surfacing major issues in living together as a multifaith family. To its credit, the staff has never considered abandoning its efforts to find a way to be together in prayer and meditation. Its efforts have proven that a multifaith staff can not only work together as an integrated unity, but can share their faith on an intimate level without offending each other or compromising their own beliefs.

FUNDING

Becoming financially viable was a great challenge. The client medical facilities were used to the "missionary model" in which the different faith groups sent clergy (chaplains) to "see their own flocks." Consequently, the "contributions" by the medical facilities only made up eight percent of The Chaplaincy's total budget.

After 1983 the Co-Presidents persuaded medical facility administrators that they needed to treat certified chaplains as their other professional staff members if they wanted to truly integrate spiritual care into the therapeutic environment. Even if only for the public relations benefit, spiritual care needed to be elevated to department status. When The Chaplaincy made the commitment to become multifaith and, as partners, to raise the counterpart funds to provide the student chaplains, the medical facilities began to establish departments of pastoral care and education and take responsibility for providing offices and salary support. The arrangement became the "Partnership Model," leapfrogging the stages of "employee model" and "contract model."

The marketing strategy involved approaching prospective medical facility partners and, even if they were laying off other professionals, persuading them to establish a department of pastoral care and education with an initial chaplain, or chaplains, supported by a grant obtained by The Chaplaincy. The proviso was that, if the results were as promised, the medical facility would move the position(s) into its budget in the succeeding two years.

Private individual and foundation support made up the bulk of the revenues originally, and still does. The Chaplaincy later found it could obtain grants from corporations based on the fact that the chaplains were caring for their employees and their families on a non-sectarian basis, and were making medical care more cost-effective in the process. With corporations, the solicitation vocabulary is always in terms of "health care and spiritual support" with religious terminology ("pastoral care," "sacramental," etc.) used in solicitation of individuals and religiously oriented foundations, congregations and judicatories.

While The Chaplaincy gained legitimacy in its fund-raising by alluding to its prestigious institutional partners, it has come to the point where it is well enough known in the community for the institutions to acknowledge, publicly, their pride in being associated with The Chaplaincy! Now, other institutions are coming to The Chaplaincy to inquire about forming a partnership.

The Chaplaincy bought computer software to automate the building of mailing lists and the direct mailing of individual solicitations. Through newsletters and an annual report, the personal stories of results and measures of successful growth were communicated to donors and prospective supporters. The fact that this new non-profit model was unique in the community did not hurt; no one else could come to them with the same case for support, though explaining how it worked was not always easy.

The clinical staff has gladly surrendered the primary responsibility for raising program funds. The Chaplaincy insists, however, that they participate willingly and enthusiastically in providing hospitality to visiting prospects. They also make public appearances to raise the organization's visibility and add names to the list of friends who will receive the newsletter and other mailings (a function clergy would perform in any congregation or other charitable organization).

Public events have helped raise the visibility of The Chaplaincy. For many years, supporters were considered members by asking for their votes at the annual meeting (a pro forma ritual no longer observed). Besides reporting on accomplishments, an effort is now made to provide an inspirational content to the annual meeting with music, prayers and presentations reflecting The Chaplaincy's multifaith character. Most importantly, new chaplain staff are lifted up, publicly, through an installation ceremony in which each is introduced by the administrator of the medical facility and given a brief charge by a key leader of the relevant denomination or faith group (President of the board of Rabbis, Bishop, etc.).

The Chaplaincy's most successful fund-raising event is a formal dinner that combines the interests and support of the medical facilities, the business community and its own trustees. Each partner medical facility nominates an outstanding patient care practitioner (other than a chaplain) who demonstrates respect for the whole person–body, mind and spirit. The nominee is given the "Wholeness of Life Award" with a citation written by The Chaplaincy, but read by the leader of the awardee's medical institution. All the medical facilities, of course, buy tables (sometimes two or three when a popular nurse honoree is supported by a number of doctors). At the same time, an outstanding business leader who demonstrates similar respect for persons is honored. With the help of his/her friends, acting as Co-Hosts, a number of other companies related to the leader's firm are pleased to purchase tables–and thus become introduced to The Chaplaincy. This dinner now provides 20 percent of a $4 million budget.

Contributions from the medical facilities have increased from eight percent (1983) of the budget to just over 50 percent currently. Grants and contributions cover the remaining education, research and overhead costs. As the efficacy of The Chaplaincy's program is increasingly proved, medical facilities may be persuaded to pay more of the direct costs of the education program as well as of the professional staff. Lobbying is being conducted in Washington to make the Medicare law clear in allowing Medicare providers to receive the pass-through reimbursement for the education portion when the hospitals have organized with others in a Partnership or Contract Model such as is conducted by The Chaplaincy.

THE FUTURE

The possibilities for further service in spiritual care, education and research spring from the broadening of the partnerships developed by The Chaplaincy. Here are some of them:

- We have begun support groups consisting of patients and family members from multiple partner medical facilities, i.e., bereavement groups. Patients from multiple institutions can quickly fill a group and The Chaplaincy's central facilities provide a comfortable ambiance to accommodate them.
- With a broader base of institutions, it is more feasible to train pastoral visitors to serve in medical facilities near their place of work or home.

- There are practitioners in physical and mental health professions who are eager to explore the potential of spiritual support in augmenting the effectiveness of current therapeutic modalities. Responsive seminars can be organized by drawing from a number of the partner institutions.
- Local clergy of all faiths are being gathered in the neutral ground of this multifaith center to share in exploring the pastoral challenges they face in their congregations–the venues where more innovative initiatives in preventive health care will undoubtedly be mounted.
- The potential for pastoral research is great with the possibility of cross-institutional studies. The recent addition of Dr. Larry VandeCreek to the organization as Director of Pastoral Research will strengthen this aspect of the organization.
- Emerging data in the burgeoning pastoral care research field should lead to more opportunities for professional and public education in The Chaplaincy's communities.

The Chaplaincy's board has commissioned its third strategic planning effort to explore these options and to answer the fundamental question of how the Chaplaincy can continue to grow without losing the core strengths of mutual support and collaboration that provide the current margin of excellence. Perhaps satellite centers will have to be formed to maintain the optimum staff size and provide greater ease of personal interaction. It will be important to reaffirm or redefine the mission and goals, remembering that the goal of growth is not as important as finding the best way to make skilled pastoral care and education available to the greatest number of people trying to cope with a health crisis.

SUMMARY

The Partnership Model developed by The HealthCare Chaplaincy offers a way of compensating for what can be the relatively marginal position of the chaplain in many institutions. The traditional pastoral care department, consisting of one or two chaplains, has little leverage against the budget demands of managed care, and seldom rates a priority in the list of fund-raising projects. Moreover, it can be difficult for pastoral care professionals to "toot their own horn" in getting across the cost-effective contribution made by skilled spiritual care.

In the Partnership Model, the trustees, as leaders in the community, provide a strong advocacy with the local institutions. Inevitably, they know trustees in each of the medical facilities. An institution can expect "a ministry of good words" to go forth in the community by incorporating The Chaplaincy's program of pastoral care and education. Conversely, they would suffer some public relations costs by cutting out spiritual care, given the expanding network of Chaplaincy supporters throughout the religious *and* business communities.

This positive networking comes only after the struggle to create the multi-institutional system at the outset. The Chaplaincy was, in a sense, fortunate because the prospective institutions, for the most part, did not already have pastoral care departments; that is, there were no staffs in place. Pre-existing staffs are not generally eager to make the trade-off of becoming accountable to a new authority to gain the benefits of a professional community, even in the face of increasing insecurity created by managed care. It may be easier, therefore, in creating a Partnership Model, to begin with client institutions who do not have professional departments–or who have lost their staff–and want to establish a first rate program.

In the end, it is the experience of The HealthCare Chaplaincy's staff that the additional resources, the mutual support, the increased visibility, and the resulting flexibility and diversity all make the partnership effort worthwhile. The total result is consonant with the goal of integrating skilled spiritual support and excellent clinical education in more health care settings. This promotes healing in individuals, in families, in institutions and in the community.

APPENDIX

THE HEALTHCARE CHAPLAINCY PARTNER MEDICAL FACILITIES, BY DATE OF FIRST SERVICE

1961 Lenox Hill Hospital–Manhattan, New York City

1961 Memorial Sloan-Kettering Cancer Center

1961 The New York and Presbyterian Hospital

1962 (formerly The New York Hospital-Cornell Medical Center)

1971 Hospital for Special Surgery, Manhattan, NYC

1979 Beth Israel Medical Center, North Division, Manhattan (formerly Doctors Hospital)

1981 DeWitt Nursing Home, Manhattan, NYC

1985 New York University Medical Center, Manhattan, NYC

1986 Winifred Masterson Burke Rehabilitation Hospital, White Plains, NY

1991 The New York Hospital-Cornell Medical Center, Westchester (Psychiatric) Division, White Plains, NY

1993	The New York Hospital Medical Center of Queens, NYC
1993	Lawrence Hospital, Bronxville, NY
1993	Florence Nightingale Health Center, Manhattan, NYC
1994	Ronald McDonald House, Manhattan, NYC
1995	The Beth Israel Healthcare System, Manhattan, NYC
1995	NYU Downtown Hospital, Manhattan, NYC (formerly Beekman Downtown Hospital)
1996	Griffin Hospital, Derby, CT
1997	United Hospital, Port Chester, NY
1998	Brookdale University Hospital and Medical Center, Brooklyn, NYC
1998	Nyack Hospital, Nyack, NY
1998	White Plains Hospital Center, White Plains, NY
1999	Winthrop University Hospital, Mineola, NY

Interfaith Health Care Ministries, Providence, Rhode Island

Duane Parker, PhD

HISTORY-IDENTIFY A LOCAL NEED

The Interfaith Health Care Ministries (IHCM) was incorporated in 1975 by the Diocese of Providence, Board of Rabbis, and the Rhode Island State Council of Churches. Important persons who brought this about were the Dean of the Brown University Medical School, Stanley Aronson, MD, and the University Chaplain, The Reverend Charles Baldwin. Prior to the incorporation of IHCM, the religious community provided the pastoral services through volunteers or clergy they assigned to hospital ministry.

The original IHCM proposal requested the hospitals affiliated with the medical school to employ qualified hospital chaplains. These chaplains would provide pastoral care services for patients and families as well as educational programs for medical students and area clergy. Administrators, however, objected on two grounds: (1) they believed the religious community should provide such services, and (2) it cost too much. However, religious leaders, medical school administrators, and the hospital administrators agreed that an educational program was needed in Rhode Island. They explored several options and decided to seek the employment of an ACPE certified supervisor to begin a CPE program. It was understood that the program would provide limited service and education with minimal costs. After a national search, the first director, Duane Parker, was employed in January 1976.

Rev. Duane Parker is Executive Director, Interfaith Health Care Ministries, Rhode Island Hospital, Gerry House #36, Providence, RI 02915 (E-mail: dfparker@juno.com).

[Haworth co-indexing entry note]: "Interfaith Health Care Ministries, Providence, Rhode Island." Parker, Duane. Co-published simultaneously in *Journal of Health Care Chaplaincy* (The Haworth Pastoral Press, an imprint of The Haworth Press, Inc.) Vol. 9, No. 1/2, 1999, pp. 43-48; and: *Contract Pastoral Care and Education: The Trend of the Future?* (ed: Larry VandeCreek) The Haworth Pastoral Press, an imprint of The Haworth Press, Inc., 1999, pp. 43-48. Single or multiple copies of this article are available for a fee from The Haworth Document Delivery Service [1-800-342-9678, 9:00 a.m. - 5:00 p.m. (EST). E-mail address: getinfo@haworthpressinc.com].

Since ownership of the program was unique–comprised of the interfaith community, the medical school, and seven hospitals, the ACPE regional accreditation committee did not consider IHCM to be a center. It recommended that one hospital be selected, instead of seven, and that the supervisor and program focus attention there. However, the IHCM Board disagreed and requested a decision by the ACPE National Commission. This Commission accredited the center in 1977 over the objection of the Region and the first CPE students enrolled in the program that summer. They provided pastoral care in one of the IHCM hospitals three days a week and attended seminars two days each week to reduce travel time. Since that time 500 students have completed the program.

In 1984, William Nisi became the director and he served until 1994. He developed a concept whereby interested agencies could contract with IHCM for a half-time chaplain who could then spend the other half of his time in Supervisory CPE. This concept has led to the establishment of four such positions.

There are three certified supervisors on the IHCM staff and annually 35 students complete one of the CPE programs. Current programs include a full-time (summer) and a nine-month internship with students providing pastoral care in one of the agencies while under supervision by IHCM. An extended unit is offered for area clergy who use their placement as their clinical site.

ACPE and the United States Catholic Conference (USCC) accredit the program. This was made possible through the employment of two supervisors with dual certification, Sr. Dorothy Cotterell, SUSC, and Sr. Maureen Mitchell, RSM.

ARTICULATE THE MISSION

In 1975, IHCM's mission was to provide educational programs for interested clergy, physicians, nurses, and other health care providers. The educational mission included establishing a nationally accredited clinical pastoral education program. This mission was fulfilled. In 1995 the mission was expanded to include providing both education and direct pastoral services. The mission statements evolved from the Board's evaluation of what was missing in the community and how IHCM might meet these needs.

SELECT A BOARD WILLING TO STRUGGLE AND SERVE

IHCM is a not-for-profit organization governed by an elected Board. The Board has two types of membership: agency representatives and community representatives. When an organization joins IHCM, it agrees to provide a board member, financial support, and a clinical placement for ministry. Agency representatives have the dual function of representing their agency to IHCM and IHCM to their agency.

Community representatives are elected because of their interest in the program and because they bring specific talents useful to the Board. Community members may be faculty members from universities, community leaders, or former agency representatives. Currently the Board, which numbers 26 members, meets regularly with primary responsibility for establishing policies, employing staff, and approving programs. An active and talented Board is an important key to developing a community-based program. These individuals become the agency's voice in the sponsoring agencies and wider community.

INTENTIONALLY INVOLVING THE INTERFAITH COMMUNITY

Since the religious community incorporated IHCM, two clergy from each faith community serve on the Board. However, the interfaith connection is problematic. Initially religious leaders expressed considerable interest in interfaith efforts. As these leaders were replaced, the interest has decreased. Continuing effort is required to make sure that the interfaith community claims ownership for the program. Currently, most religious leaders have come to the community within the past two years and they are being asked what they want from the IHCM program. One recent positive development was the decision of the Jewish hospital to employ a full-time chaplain rabbi through IHCM.

One complicated issue is that the Roman Catholic and Episcopal Churches provide chaplains, deacons, and eucharistic ministers to the various health care agencies in RI at no cost to the hospital. These religious leaders are being asked if they are ready to join a unified chaplaincy program and if they are willing to support the interfaith approach to obtain adequate hospital and community funding for such a program. It is not clear how this discussion will progress.

All IHCM chaplains and CPE students are assigned to their setting to represent the interfaith religious community rather than one specific faith group. They network with clergy of other faiths as required in the clinical setting.

FUNDING: START WITH WHAT YOU CAN AND GROW

IHCM started with a very modest budget, supporting a CPE supervisor with limited office services. Through the years it expanded as the program demonstrated its value in the community to a current budget of almost a half million dollars.

In the beginning, administrators wanted IHCM to seek start-up grants. The Board decided, however, that solid financial support had to come from the original agencies if it was to succeed. We have received only two modest foundation grants in our history. One was from the Rhode Island Foundation that gave program money and one from the Robert Wood Johnson Foundation to begin consumer-run drop-in centers for mentally ill individuals seeking community integration.

Our fund-raising efforts are complicated by the fact that we are a shadow program in another agency. Therefore, contributors will give a gift to hospice rather than to our organization although they are grateful for the chaplaincy services. Our sponsoring agencies do not want us competing with their fund-raising efforts. Based upon the IHCM experience it is good to begin small with limited resources and grow slowly as funds increase.

OFFER A UNIQUE PRODUCT

Our staff and Board continually wrestle with the question, "What is the product we offer and who are the clients?" The question is easier to articulate than to answer. Currently we offer three unique products: educational programs, pastoral services, and a network for the religious community and health care agencies. We briefly discuss each below.

CPE is the primary educational product. However, we are also involved with physicians in a medical school committee to integrate spirituality into the curriculum and co-teach courses on Cancer and Ethics as well as Spirituality in Medicine. Several medical students are interested in a CPE experience so that they can explore what happens to them in their clinical rotations. Plans are being developed to conduct a major conference on spirituality in medicine. In addition, we are involved in teaching a course titled "Integrating Spirituality in Professional Practice" through the University of Rhode Island Nursing Continuing Education program.

We provide pastoral services in four hospitals, two hospice programs, two eldercare programs, and a community mental health center. Interfaith will soon begin a new program at the state hospital that provides general and psychiatric services. In addition, our extended CPE students serve in prisons, parishes, and other community agencies such as a woman's shelter.

Our third product is networking with community agencies. Our most recent effort is developing a program involving mental health consumers, family members, mental health professionals, and area clergy. The program has developed four consumer-run drop-in centers hosted by faith communities, providing bi-annual worship services, and participating in advocacy efforts. Key to these efforts is our insistence that representatives from all these divergent communities be involved in program planning.

KEEP THE INTERNAL STRUCTURE SIMPLE AND FLEXIBLE

We strive to keep our structure simple and flexible. Since we are small, this is possible although recent growth has required more structure. The Board employs a Director with responsibilities to oversee the program. A part-time office manager serves as the communication link between all parts of the program. Supervisors provide CPE through the center, provide administration, and care in one of the sponsoring agencies.

THE FUTURE IS ALWAYS UNKNOWN

IHCM faces five major challenges as it moves into the future. They are:

- maintaining interfaith community support;
- continued funding by sponsoring agencies and increasing fund-raising efforts;
- significant involvement at the medical school, nursing school, theological school, and other educational programs;
- linking health and interfaith religious communities as health care continues moving to the community; and
- providing a flexible CPE program designed to meet local needs.

We are meeting these challenges by developing a strategic plan and focusing Board committees on specific tasks to meet these challenges. Since the majority of the CPE students are serving in the community, IHCM is in a unique position to provide the networking required in the new health care milieu.

WHAT HAVE WE LEARNED THAT COULD BE HELPFUL TO OTHERS?

Through our twenty-four year history we have learned the following about developing a community-based pastoral care/education program.

- Identify a local community need.
- Articulate a mission statement to serve as a roadmap.
- Be visionary and committed to fulfill the vision.
- Recruit and develop a strong board committed to the organization's mission.

- Obtain commitments for adequate funds hopefully for at least three years.
- Network with community agency representatives, area clergy, and consumers.
- Recruit qualified, dedicated, and flexible staff.

SUMMARY

We enjoy considerable freedom in the creation of programs that meet the spiritual needs of people in the community. We minister in diverse settings–a university medical school, hospital, hospice, eldercare center, mental health center, state hospital, and parish/congregation. We are guided by our deep commitment to make sure that individuals and families whose life journey is hard receive quality spiritual care. We are equally committed to preparing caregivers, whether clergy, physicians, nurses, or laypersons so that they are both clinically competent and spiritually informed. Our ambitions are high and our resources are limited.

Lutheran Chaplaincy Service, Cleveland, Ohio

Richard D. Warger, MDiv

SUMMARY OF MISSION

"Being empowered by the Gospel, the mission of Lutheran Chaplaincy Service is to bring the promise of hope, healing, wholeness and balance to persons experiencing the blessings and brokenness of human life."

HISTORY

Lutheran Chaplaincy Service was founded in 1914 as part of a Lutheran city mission movement emerging in a number of cities after the turn of the century. Although the leadership of the organization was initially limited to men, women served in the ministry as early as the 1920s. In the late 1920s, the organization ceased its congregational work and concentrated solely on its institutional ministry. Over the succeeding thirty years, a number of pastors served as chaplains to a multitude of municipal and private institutions. The ministry itself focused on brief contacts with many people in a large number of institutions: 40 or more institutions were served by no more than four chaplains. In the 1950s, the Lutheran Service Society of Northern Ohio (LSSNO) was established by two smaller Lutheran church bodies. Although designed for more comprehensive services, the LSSNO essentially provided chaplaincy services to institutions not

---

Rev. Richard D. Warger is Executive Director, Lutheran Chaplaincy Service, 4100 Franklin Avenue, Cleveland, OH 44113 (E-mail: lcs@spiritualcare.org).

[Haworth co-indexing entry note]: "Lutheran Chaplaincy Service, Cleveland, Ohio." Warger, Richard D. Co-published simultaneously in *Journal of Health Care Chaplaincy* (The Haworth Pastoral Press, an imprint of The Haworth Press, Inc.) Vol. 9, No. 1/2, 1999, pp. 49-57; and: *Contract Pastoral Care and Education: The Trend of the Future?* (ed: Larry VandeCreek) The Haworth Pastoral Press, an impinrt of The Haworth Press, Inc., 1999, pp. 49-57. Single or multiple copies of this article are available for a fee from The Haworth Document Delivery Service [1-800-342-9678, 9:00 a.m. - 5:00 p.m. (EST). E-mail address: getinfo@haworthpressinc.com].

served by the Lutheran Chaplaincy Service (then called Lutheran Institutional Ministry Society). In 1974, the two organizations merged to become the Lutheran Chaplaincy Service of Greater Cleveland.

During the 1970s, the organization failed to adapt to a number of environmental changes, including the need for better resource development, increased expectations for pastoral care services, higher standards for certification of chaplains, and the need for a Board of Trustees able to deal with more sophisticated issues. Consequently, by the end of 1980, Lutheran Chaplaincy Service had no staff but was developing new leadership and shaping a new vision. In 1981, guided by the new vision and leadership, the organization placed, for the first time through formal contractual arrangements, three full-time chaplains in community institutions. This partnership assured support and income from the institutions while Lutheran Chaplaincy Service assured quality pastoral care and professional support for the chaplains. Continued growth and contracts occurred during the 1980s, with two significant changes occurring in the late 1980s. In 1987, Lutheran Chaplaincy Service placed its first chaplain outside of Greater Cleveland. In 1989, the first non-Lutheran chaplain joined the staff.

Currently, Lutheran Chaplaincy Service serves eighteen different institutions and/or programs in northeastern Ohio with twenty-one full-time and three part-time chaplains representing twelve denominations. It provides a comprehensive program of emotional and spiritual care services to community institutions, particularly health care institutions. Regardless of denominational identity, emotional and spiritual support services are offered to people of all segments of society. Lutheran Chaplaincy Service has been the initiator and provider of spiritual care services in community institutions throughout northeastern Ohio. This educational and developmental effort has been on the cutting edge of emerging medical and health care studies and discoveries that have attested to the critical importance of emotional and spiritual issues to the health and well-being of people.

As Lutheran Chaplaincy Service has progressed in the early 1990s, it has done so in the midst of a rapidly changing demographic, economic, and health care environment. These changes spurred the need for the organization to develop a strategic, long-range plan to guide it during the last half of the decade and position it for continued success in the next century. This process produced goals and strategies designed to respond to critical issues facing Lutheran Chaplaincy Service and to renew the vision and mission of the organization for the future.

BOARD OF DIRECTORS

The original Board in 1914 was made up of local Lutheran pastors and laymen. They were recruited from congregations of the Lutheran

Church–Missouri Synod. From that time to the early 1980s Board members continued to be recruited from the member Lutheran congregations. The two major changes in those years were the addition of congregations from other Lutheran church bodies and recruitment of women as Board members. A third change was the recruitment of Board members from other Christian denominations.

Currently, Board members are recruited from Christian denominations. The Executive Committee of the Board serves as the nominating committee. The committee seeks to recruit individuals who have a variety of personal and professional skills that will enable the Board to address the many complex issues facing non-profit agencies. Professions represented can include: attorneys, financial management experts, health care administrators, clergy and consumers.

The Board of Directors of Lutheran Chaplaincy Service is a working board. All Board members receive committee assignments and are expected to attend all meetings of the Board and committees. All new Board members receive a job description for Board members and a set of guidelines and expectations for board membership. The most critical and active committees are the Executive, Finance and Personnel. Members of the Personnel Committee are directly involved in interviews of candidates for chaplaincy positions and the selection process. The Finance Committee regularly monitors financial records and reporting, planning and procedures. They also oversee the management of the small endowment. The Executive Committee conducts the official business of the organization between the bi-monthly Board meetings, oversees program planning and responds to organizational issues that arise.

INTERFAITH RELATIONSHIPS

Relationships with the interfaith community have been primarily programmatic rather than formal, that is, there are no formal relationships between Lutheran Chaplaincy Service and any denomination or faith group other than the Lutheran Church bodies. However, Board members are recruited from other denominations. There are no significant pastoral care initiatives in the local Jewish or Muslim communities in our service area, although our chaplains make connections with clergy from these faith communities as the needs of patients are identified.

Twelve Christian denominations are represented on the current staff of Lutheran Chaplaincy Service. This began in the late 1980s with a philosophical commitment to selecting and placing the best possible candidates. This was a change from the previous history of only hiring Lutheran men. There have been no difficulties with this diversity. The tremendous advantage is that the diversity in faith traditions conflates into a common mission of compassion and care. A great deal of sharing and learning occurs between the chaplains as they explore how their differing backgrounds can enhance everyone's ministry.

START-UP FUNDING

Lutheran Chaplaincy Service has such a long history that start-up funding at the beginning is irrelevant to today. Even in 1981 when the period of renewal began, there was continuing funding from local congregations. It was enough to allow the development of our current model, although funds remained very tight throughout the 1980s into the early 1990s. Development of contractual relationships with institutions was the only way to make the ministry both viable and sustainable. Initially in 1981, LCS established contracts with institutions that covered at least 80% of the cost of the chaplain's salary and benefits. The remainder was covered by charitable funds, primarily from congregations, but also from individuals. Beginning in 1983, we began establishing new contracts that covered 100% of the cost of the chaplain, plus an administrative fee to defray some, but not all, of the overhead. Today sixteen of our eighteen contracts are cost plus administrative fee. Our oldest two contracts cover 100% of the cost without the administrative fee. In 1998, 86% of income will come from program revenue.

It seems to me that it is possible to begin a new pastoral care agency with adequate initial funding. It could begin as a subsidiary organization of an existing service agency or as a corporation owned by several church judicatories or religious service organizations. I believe that a minimum investment of up to $50,000 per year for up to five years would provide an opportunity to develop sustainability. However, I also believe there are several key factors that must be addressed:

1. A committed Board of Directors is absolutely essential. Composition of the Board should not be limited to clergy and "church folks" but include a diversity of professionals with a compassionate heart for the ministry.
2. The selection of the ministry developer is absolutely critical. This individual must have a working knowledge of pastoral care ministry, basic business principles, sales skills and an entrepreneurial spirit. Interestingly, I do not believe that the person necessarily needs four units of CPE and chaplaincy experience.
3. A fund development program should be initiated as soon as possible after incorporation. Together, the Board and developer can begin to establish relationships that have the potential to provide charitable support.

GOVERNMENTAL RELATIONSHIPS

Lutheran Chaplaincy Service has had limited relationships with governmental agencies. We have not pursued contracts with the state or federal corrections systems, primarily because they tend to have their own system for chaplaincy. Such systems typically operate very differently from a nonprofit, faith-based organization. We have had a contract with the local county for a full-time juvenile correction chaplain. Such a contract is generally more complex and requires more levels of political processing than the usual contract with a private, nonprofit institution. In our case, the contract requires going through the same extensive renewal process each year. Each year the possibility exists that the changing political environment may impact the renewal. Our other contracts are more typically three years in length and generally have an automatic renewal clause that will continue service unless written termination notice is given within a prescribed time period. However, our size allows us to consider governmental contracts. We are currently developing a proposal with a department of the county government.

Governmental contracts have several disadvantages for a newer organization. First, they are more time-consuming to develop, with the outcome still subject to the vagaries of the political system that have no relation to the merits of the contract or position. Second, an organization that contracts predominantly with governmental entities could have a large part of its program eliminated due to shifting political priorities. Finally, management of the contracts may be more time-consuming than those with private, nonprofit or proprietary institutions. My advice would be to establish a track record with the latter organizations before investing substantial time in the development of governmental contracts. However, having stated this caveat, I always recommend practicing "creative opportunism." By this I mean to suggest evaluating each opportunity thoroughly to determine not only the service and financial aspects but also to determine if it offers any long-term strategic advantage or would establish a connection that could lead to other opportunities or support for the chaplaincy organization.

MARKETING

The product Lutheran Chaplaincy Service offers is a comprehensive pastoral care program. We can offer as much or as little as an institution needs or desires. Our primary mission goal is to see that community institutions have excellent pastoral care. Since we are mission-driven we do not wait for opportunities to emerge, we also work to create opportunities where we determine that a quality spiritual care program can enhance an institution or community. Thus, we will both approach institutions with our services *and* work with clergy and community leaders who may be able to influence the institution's management. The administrations of the institutions we serve are used as references, both passively (listed in our materials) and actively (administrators contacting their peers).

The services we offer have flexible levels. As a charitable, mission-driven organization, the level of service has little effect on income. One of our goals is to optimize each institution's experience with pastoral care through Lutheran Chaplaincy Service. As flexible as our services can be, they can be grouped in basic categories.

1. *Comprehensive*–Our comprehensive services are designed primarily for institutions who have no or little experience with clinical pastoral care. We begin by educating administration and developing a team of institutional staff members who represent the diverse professions and departments of the institution. With this team, we begin the creation of the pastoral care program. This not only educates and prepares institutional personnel for the introduction of pastoral care, it provides the material for development of a job description specifically for the needs of this particular institution. It also creates ownership of the program among the various departments and professions represented on the team. Concurrent with this, we conduct a national search for candidates. We provide the institution with a list of several quality candidates. Interviews are conducted by the institution's team and our Personnel Committee. A mutually agreed upon selection is made. The spiritual care provider is placed and functions within the structure of the institution but is our employee. We provide quality assurance to the institution and peer support for the chaplain.
2. *Renewal*–In situations in which an institution is replacing a chaplain of their own employ, we conduct a streamlined version of the comprehensive process and add the quality assurance and peer support components.
3. *Search and Interview*–For a fee we will consider doing the development and search process without the continuing contract. Although no institutions have selected this option, it would be similar to the comprehensive services, except that the institution would hire the chaplain and we would not provide on-going quality assurance and peer support. Our relationship with the institution would end after the chaplain was selected and hired.
4. *Consultation*–We also offer several types of consulting services. (1) We assess and analyze the spiritual care needs of an institution or organization and make recommendations. (2) We consult with interested community or church groups who wish to develop a structural model for spiritual care ministry similar to ours. (3) We review candidates for

pastoral care positions and conduct a reference process. These services are generally provided out-of-state or outside of our service area.

ORGANIZATIONAL STRUCTURE

Lutheran Chaplaincy Service is a nonprofit corporation owned by congregations. We are affiliated with Lutheran Services in America as part of its $3 billion social ministry network. Several denominations are represented on our Board of Directors. The organization is managed by an executive director, associate director and an administrative assistant. Each chaplain has an office in his or her respective institution and location. Since chaplains are located over a sizable service area, we would fit management expert Henry Minzberg's definition of a dispersed professional bureaucracy. In essence, our structure is web-like as depicted in our organizational chart (Figure 1).

The chaplains are all employees of Lutheran Chaplaincy Service. We maintain a comprehensive benefits package that includes health coverage, pension, long- and short-term disability and life insurance. We carry an umbrella insurance policy that covers each chaplain for liability. This is generally required by our contracted institutions. We maintain a personnel policy that serves as the default when an institution does not have a policy. However, we work with our contract institutions to strongly encourage adopting our vacation policy of four weeks.

THE FUTURE

For years I have been listening to distress from chaplains who are worried about positions disappearing through downsizing. However, where that has occurred, it seems to me, is where there was limited vision. Those chaplains who have lost jobs have adapted and found new ones if they had vision and could see beyond the boundaries of the traditional pastoral care paradigm.

The future is ours to create. There is a growing rather than shrinking need for spiritual care support. Specifically, I see many opportunities to share our gifts of ministry throughout our communities and society. Without limiting the vision, several specific areas are evident.

The first is the creation of a continuum of care. One of the greatest frustrations a chaplain can have is working with a patient or family and then have them discharged with much pastoral care left to do. We have the opportunity to develop collaborative models with congregations and community service providers to see that people have access to continuing care after their contact with the chaplain in the institutions. We are currently exploring several initiatives.

FIGURE 1

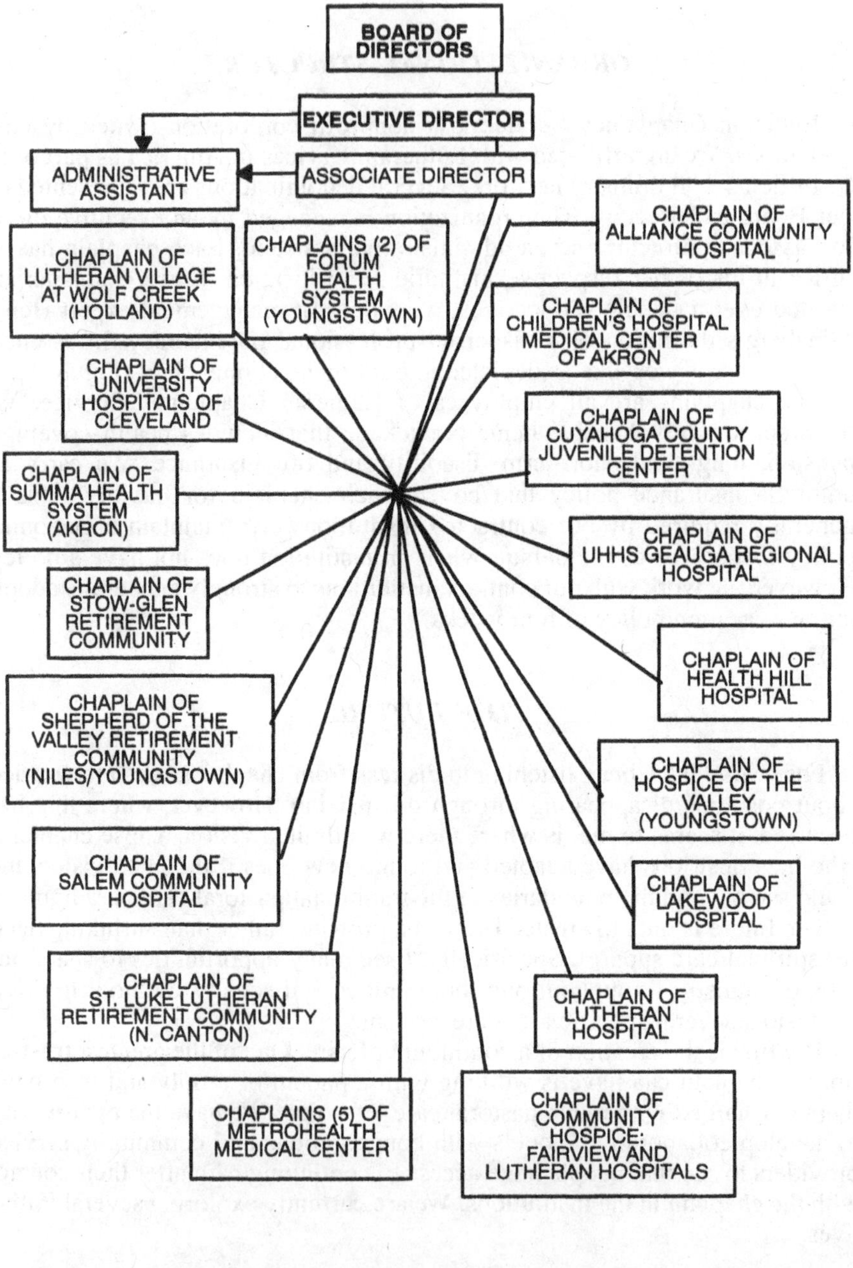
BOARD OF DIRECTORS
EXECUTIVE DIRECTOR
ADMINISTRATIVE ASSISTANT
ASSOCIATE DIRECTOR
CHAPLAIN OF ALLIANCE COMMUNITY HOSPITAL
CHAPLAIN OF LUTHERAN VILLAGE AT WOLF CREEK (HOLLAND)
CHAPLAINS (2) OF FORUM HEALTH SYSTEM (YOUNGSTOWN)
CHAPLAIN OF CHILDREN'S HOSPITAL MEDICAL CENTER OF AKRON
CHAPLAIN OF UNIVERSITY HOSPITALS OF CLEVELAND
CHAPLAIN OF CUYAHOGA COUNTY JUVENILE DETENTION CENTER
CHAPLAIN OF SUMMA HEALTH SYSTEM (AKRON)
CHAPLAIN OF UHHS GEAUGA REGIONAL HOSPITAL
CHAPLAIN OF STOW-GLEN RETIREMENT COMMUNITY
CHAPLAIN OF HEALTH HILL HOSPITAL
CHAPLAIN OF SHEPHERD OF THE VALLEY RETIREMENT COMMUNITY (NILES/YOUNGSTOWN)
CHAPLAIN OF HOSPICE OF THE VALLEY (YOUNGSTOWN)
CHAPLAIN OF SALEM COMMUNITY HOSPITAL
CHAPLAIN OF LAKEWOOD HOSPITAL
CHAPLAIN OF ST. LUKE LUTHERAN RETIREMENT COMMUNITY (N. CANTON)
CHAPLAIN OF LUTHERAN HOSPITAL
CHAPLAINS (5) OF METROHEALTH MEDICAL CENTER
CHAPLAIN OF COMMUNITY HOSPICE: FAIRVIEW AND LUTHERAN HOSPITALS

The other side of the continuum of care is wellness, health and the creation of healthy communities. Many of the discussions of spirituality and health have left out the traditional pastoral care model. We have the opportunity to contribute to the discussion and to the initiatives and in doing so, discovering a deeper richness in our ministry. More immediate initiatives, several of which we are exploring, can be a workplace chaplaincy, clergy and professional support and care, collaboration with other community caregiving organizations. Within the next five years I hope and expect to see that Lutheran Chaplaincy Service is participating in and contributing to a much broader continuum of care and health.

GENERAL ADVICE

The best thing we did in our developmental years was to value what we have to offer. We have continued to refine our articulation of both the value of spiritual care services and the added value of the Lutheran Chaplaincy Service model. Our reputation is built on the quality of our relationships with the institutions we serve. The institutional administrators have become our primary references as we continue to grow.

A second strong positive emphasis has been the relationships within our peer support structure. Each chaplain knows that the Associate Director or myself is available to respond to any concerns they may have. In addition, the relationship that each chaplain establishes with the other chaplains through our regular staff meetings not only provides support but also shared expertise that can enhance their respective ministries. The organizational chart does not show the web connections between the chaplains but they are there, strengthening ministries and building allegiance to our common culture of compassion within Lutheran Chaplaincy Service. These relationships transcend any issues around denominational differences.

Our positive experiences are the result of strong relationships around service and mutual vision. Our weaknesses are the result of not establishing enough relationships around resource development. We have been less adept at developing funding resources through grant writing and planned as well as deferred giving. A long-term development plan can be as important as creating initial funding for an organization like ours and particularly for one organizing in today's environment.

One suggestion is to be willing to take calculated risks for the sake of the mission. If a group is authentically committed to seeing that excellent spiritual care services are available, it will be willing to risk even its existence to reach its goal. A second suggestion is to look beyond the traditional pastoral care model. Dream and envision all the places in our world where distressed souls seek spiritual care and discover where you can respond.

The McFarland Institute, Inc., New Orleans, Louisiana

E. W. Huffstutler, Jr., MDiv

SUMMARY OF MISSION

The McFarland Institute ("The Institute") is operated by Christian Health Ministries whose mission is "to educate ministers and laypersons in the clinical arts of pastoral care and counseling and in the importance of the spiritual dimension of healing." It also promotes physical and spiritual health and wholeness in the community.

The Institute, through the divisions of Clinical Pastoral Education and Pastoral Counseling, operates ACPE and AAPC accredited training programs. The clinical sites for these programs include four major hospitals, the New Orleans Police Department, five smaller institutions including a nursing home, a children's hospital, two smaller medical facilities, five local parishes, six social service agencies, and a pastoral counseling center.

We train approximately 100 students in these clinical sites, providing pastoral care services and therapy for institutions, individuals and the community at large. The Institute enjoys academic affiliations with three local seminaries and the University of New Orleans.

In addition to formal training programs, The Institute sponsors or co-sponsors 10-15 seminars for the community per year. These range from the Madden Seminar, named for Myron Madden, Ph.D. (long-time Director of Pastoral Care at Southern Baptist Hospital), which focuses on pastoral care or

---

Rev. E. W. Huffstutler, Jr., is Executive Director, The McFarland Institute, Inc., 1450 Poydras Street, Suite 1550, New Orleans, LA 70112 (E-mail: ghuffstutler@TMCFI.org).

[Haworth co-indexing entry note]: "The McFarland Institute, Inc., New Orleans, Louisiana." Huffstutler, E. W., Jr. Co-published simultaneously in *Journal of Health Care Chaplaincy* (The Haworth Pastoral Press, an imprint of The Haworth Press, Inc.) Vol. 9, No. 1/2, 1999, pp. 59-65; and: *Contract Pastoral Care and Education: The Trend of the Future?* (ed: Larry VandeCreek) The Haworth Pastoral Press, an imprint of The Haworth Press, Inc., 1999, pp. 59-65. Single or multiple copies of this article are available for a fee from The Haworth Document Delivery Service [1-800-342-9678, 9:00 a.m. - 5:00 p.m. (EST). E-mail address: getinfo@haworthpressinc.com].

clinical pastoral education issues, to the Spring Lectures in Pastoral Counseling. Each of these seminars is designed to expand the interface between physical and spiritual healing.

HISTORY

In the early 1920s, denominational hospitals were springing up all over the United States. Southern Baptists were beginning to consider seriously building hospitals as a means of evangelism and service. At that same time, in New Orleans a "city missionary," Clementine Kelley, examined the needs of the city. She discovered a metropolis with 1,500 hospital beds that needed 4,000. To her, this represented the greatest need of the city and the greatest opportunity for Baptists.

It was Clementine Kelley's vision that led to the founding of Southern Baptist Hospital in 1924. Pastoral Care was always a part of that vision of health care. Dr. W. W. Hamilton, a former president of the Southern Baptist Convention, was the first Chaplain. In 1960, Myron Madden became Chaplain. Madden was a principal in the New Orleans branch of the Southern Baptist Association for Clinical Pastoral Education, one of the organizations that formed the Association for Clinical Pastoral Education. Over nearly 25 years, he built the Pastoral Care Department into one of the premier clinical training programs in the South and Southwest. In addition to the hundreds of chaplains Madden trained (many who went on to become clinical educators and department heads themselves), Madden also established a Pastoral Counseling Center. The Center was accredited as a Service Center by the American Association for Pastoral Counseling in 1983.

By 1995, however, a great deal of change had occurred. Madden retired and the program he founded shrunk. New Orleans experienced the onset of new Medicare reimbursement rules (Diagnostically Related Groupings) followed by the various stages of managed care. Southern Baptist Hospital merged with Mercy Hospital, operated by the Religious Sisters of Mercy, to form Mercy † Baptist Medical Center to gain more market share. New Orleans evolved into a city with 6,000 hospital beds and only needed 3,000.

After years of attempted consolidation, it became apparent the "not-for-profit" hospitals were not moving toward greater cooperation. The decision was made by the Board of Trustees and management of Mercy † Baptist to sell the Medical Center. The Baptists chose to continue a strong ministry to New Orleans through two programs: (1) a private grant-making organization to improve the health of the overall community, and (2) a school for clinical training of ministers. The school is known today as The McFarland Institute (a Division of Christian Health Ministries).

Needs surveys showed there were only four full-time chaplaincy programs in the 23 hospitals in the city. In a city that had supported four CPE programs at one time, there was now only one. Christian Health Ministries applied for non-profit status as a school and was granted IRS approval in the summer of 1996. The McFarland Institute was formed and named after C. E. and D. A. McFarland, who over the years had generously supported Southern Baptist Hospital. Christian Health Ministries Foundation, that formerly supported the hospital, now supports The McFarland Institute. E. W. Huffstutler, who was the Director of Pastoral Care and Counseling for Southern Baptist Hospital, and later Mercy † Baptist Medical Center, was appointed the Executive Director of The McFarland Institute. Byron Harrell, former CEO of Southern Baptist Hospital and Mercy † Baptist, became President and CEO of Christian Health Ministries as well as Baptist Community Ministries (a related private grant-making organization). Charles Young continued to serve as president of Christian Health Ministries Foundation.

TRUSTEES

The Board of Trustees of Christian Health Ministries that operates The McFarland Institute is composed of the same individuals serving Baptist Community Ministries–the "parent" company. This arrangement provides a strong representative cross-section of community residents to both companies. Many of the Trustees served on the Board of the hospital before it was sold. They possess the full range of expertise and experience to oversee the expanded range of activities The Institute represents. The disadvantage to this arrangement is the division of interests between the two organizations leading to a complex and often confusing agenda. The Christian Health Ministries Board meets monthly.

Christian Health Ministries Foundation that raises money for The Institute has a Board of 45 members. The Foundation's primary efforts are publicizing The Institute, cultivating prospective donors, encouraging deferred gifts, and conducting an annual fund-raising event known as the "Spring Garden Party." The Foundation's challenge is the transition from raising money for a very visible and tangible institution–a hospital–to fund-raising for a less tangible and visible school. The Board of Trustees for Christian Health Ministries Foundation meets quarterly.

Both Trustee groups, having served a Christian hospital in the Baptist tradition, are intentionally inclusive of Baptist representatives. However, many other Christian denominations are represented among the Trustees and every effort is made to be inclusive of the various racial, ethnic, and religious traditions in the Greater New Orleans Area.

In addition, The Institute is served by a Visiting Committee including representatives from within the community and from other areas of the country having special expertise in either pastoral care or counseling. The Visiting Committee serves an advisory and consultative function for both the faculty of The Institute and for the Board of Trustees of Christian Health Ministries. The Visiting Committee meets at least twice a year and two sub-committees meet more often. The Visiting Committee, through the chairperson, reports directly to the Trustees on an annual basis, evaluating every aspect of The Institute and making recommendations for Trustee consideration.

ACTIVITIES

As a tax-exempt school, the focus of The McFarland Institute is education. In formative stages, The Institute gave careful consideration to the employment of staff chaplains and contract counselors. After a great deal of discussion with legal counsel, the decision was made to keep the current staff chaplains and contract counselors as a minor activity but not to expand beyond this limited group. These persons represent seasoned practitioners who, in addition to faculty, model the professional formation and skills being taught to McFarland interns, students, and residents.

With a new, purely educational focus, work started immediately to obtain training center status for the Pastoral Counseling Center. This meant a shift in emphasis–from service with education as a secondary activity, to education with service as by-product. In the spring of 1998, the American Association for Pastoral Counseling re-accredited the Pastoral Counseling Center as a service center and granted training center status as well. The Pastoral Counseling Division now employs four pastoral counseling interns. As an intern, a student may work on certification as a pastoral counselor (with AAPC), as a marriage and family therapist (with AAMFT), a licensed professional counselor (with the state), or as a social worker. Certified supervision is provided in each track. A counselor, otherwise qualified, may also work on more than one track.

Clinical Pastoral Education expanded from the Baptist campus of Memorial Medical Center, now a part of the Tenet Healthcare System, to the Mercy campus as well. East Jefferson General Hospital, a major provider in suburban New Orleans, added a supervisor and residents to begin a pastoral care program in 1998. In addition, a specialty is available whereby persons with a year of CPE may be placed in an institution to begin pastoral services while under supervision. Contracts with five smaller institutions are part of the training programs in order for each facility to have a chaplain four days a week. One day each week, the chaplain is engaged in educational activities. A supervisor visits each clinical site weekly and meets regularly with an administrative liaison.

The CPE program in the five smaller organizations illustrates the goal of The McFarland Institute: to serve students and the community. The student receives an opportunity to be a single chaplain–entirely responsible for pastoral care in an institution–while getting appropriate supervision and didactic support. The institution receives quality pastoral care–often cheaper than "hiring their own." If an institution likes a particular individual, however, they are welcome to hire him/her with the blessings of The McFarland Institute.

In the fall of 1998, through a contract with the Greater New Orleans Federation of Churches, The Institute began a unique program of CPE in the New Orleans Police Department. A CPE Supervisor is on staff and residents have been selected to serve as chaplains to the Police Department while participating in the CPE program. The Police program represents an opportunity not only to make a difference in the community but also to help train chaplains in law enforcement.

In addition to fully accredited programs, The Institute sponsors or co-sponsors numerous seminars in the community for professionals and laypersons. Seven seminars were presented in 1997-98.

STRUCTURE

As previously indicated, The Institute contains two divisions: (1) Clinical Pastoral Education, and (2) Pastoral Counseling, each managed by a Director with responsibility for overseeing the activities in his/her respective area. The Pastoral Counseling division includes a Clinical Director and Social Work Supervisor and may soon add personnel to work with congregations and clergy. The Clinical Pastoral Education division includes five and one-half full-time faculty.

The leadership of each division meets bimonthly along with a monthly faculty meeting. There are two planning retreats–one in the spring focussing on planning and budget preparation and another in the fall oriented toward team-building and specific needs.

The Executive Director of The McFarland Institute, in addition to Division Directors, meets with institutional representatives from the various clinical sites to discuss establishing new programs or the evaluation of existing programs. Other duties include working with Trustees in both policy setting and fund-raising activities.

McFarland employees have a loyalty to both the clinical site and to the Institute and this has been a source of some confusion. However, most have grown more comfortable with the ambiguity and are able to identify with both. Recipients of services would not recognize this duality of interests.

FUNDING

From the outset, The McFarland Institute has operated clinical sites under the terms of written contracts. The terms of the sale of Mercy † Baptist Medical Center to Tenet Healthcare, Inc. call for Pastoral Services to continue "at the same level as prior to the sale" for five years. In return for this service, Tenet provides space and physical support for pastoral services. The earliest contracts for clinical training with other institutions called for increasing financial support for services over a three-year period. The institution (in the third year) pays for all direct costs. The financial support of Christian Health Ministries and a grant from Baptist Community Ministries made this gradual assumption of costs by contract institutions possible. The Institute, however, is now at a stage wherein any additional programs must be cost-neutral, i.e., each program must pay for itself.

Even on a cost basis, The Institute provides a bargain to institutions. The Institute bears recruiting expenses and provides benefits for all employees. The direct service students provide is excellent–due to the quality of persons recruited and the supervision received. The volume of service and visibility is also increased.

THE FUTURE

Two new CPE programs bear future promise. These are both parish based and community based. Each was offered for the first time in the summer of 1998. Four seminarians completed clinical work in local congregations and six worked in local social service agencies.

The local Roman Catholic archdiocese is utilizing Institute faculty in the training of permanent deacons–many of whom will be assigned to institutional chaplaincy positions. Pastoral Counseling division faculty teach classes at the University of New Orleans in exchange for University of New Orleans faculty time with students and staff.

Marketing The Institute, for recruiting and fund-raising purposes, is also an ongoing task. However, some very creative approaches are being used, particularly in advertising the services provided by the Pastoral Counseling Center. In addition to radio and a smattering of television ads, the Center uses ads on buses, which have attracted a good deal of notice. Referral sources are tracked on all new counselees and the "ad campaign" has produced a 40% increase! Implementing a professionally designed marketing plan is important to starting new programs, recruiting students and faculty, and attracting counselees.

The first McFarland Institute Research Resident was employed in the fall of 1998. The resident is conducting research in the spiritual dimension of counseling and in health care–to the end that additional evidence of the importance of the spiritual aspect of healing will be developed. More needs to be done.

Also, a bequest funded an endowment establishing a specialty residency in oncology chaplaincy. The Rosenthal Resident provides pastoral care to oncology patients and, in addition to CPE activities, attends at least two conferences a year–at Sloan-Kettering and M. D. Anderson Hospitals. Other such specialty positions are a possibility.

Each of these programs is in very early development and requires further attention. There remain many institutions in the region without pastoral services, so the development of new programs is a continuing challenge.

The Pastoral Counseling Center is planning to develop specialized services to pastors and congregations experiencing difficulty. This program will take advantage of the special status of the Center of being pastoral without being connected to a particular faith community. Six judicatories have indicated willingness to work with the Center and to make referrals.

As one of two CPE Centers in Louisiana and the only Pastoral Counseling training program between Houston and Birmingham, The McFarland Institute has a regional presence and, perhaps, responsibility. The development of programs and/or contracts with institutions outside the Greater New Orleans Area is a future possibility.

SUMMARY

In less than three years, The McFarland Institute has grown from the equivalent of a single hospital department to a school of pastoral care and counseling serving over 100 students and 18 different institutions. It remains to be seen whether the community will support the education and service provided through grants and donations. If additional funding is secured, there are unlimited opportunities for learning and service in New Orleans and in the surrounding region.

Marketplace Ministries, Inc., Dallas, Texas

Art Stricklin, BA

HISTORY

Marketplace Ministries Inc. (MMI) of Dallas, Texas has offered Corporate Chaplain services since 1984 to businesses across the nation as a unique pro-active, personalized faith-based Employee Assistance Program (EAP).

Marketplace Ministries applies a distinctive approach that emphasizes care and compassion in the work place. Chaplains enable employers to care for the needs of employees and their family members on and off the job, 24 hours a day. This EAP serves businesses of any size, or type, with its Corporate Chaplain service, helping employees and their family members cope with the stress of daily life at work, at home and at leisure.

Marketplace Ministries began January 1, 1984, with one Chaplain, Founder and President Gil A. Stricklin, and one company of 150 employees. Today, Marketplace Ministries has a staff of 600 men and women, Hispanics, Vietnamese, Afro-Americans, and Caucasians. The chaplains and support personnel serve client companies in 369 locations caring for approximately 140,000 employees and family members across America.

The idea behind Marketplace Ministries came from Mr. Stricklin's long-time experience in the U.S. military as a chaplain from which he retired as a full colonel in 1994. There, he first learned to use the model of low-key, non-confrontational caring and compassion to service men and women across our nation.

Art Stricklin is Director of Ministry Relations, Marketplace Ministries, Inc., 12900 Preston Road, Suite 1215, Dallas, TX 75230 (National HQ E-mail: mmihq@marketplaceministries.com) (National HQ WEBSITE: www.marketplaceministries.com).

[Haworth co-indexing entry note]: "Marketplace Ministries, Inc., Dallas, Texas." Stricklin, Art. Co-published simultaneously in *Journal of Health Care Chaplaincy* (The Haworth Pastoral Press, an imprint of The Haworth Press, Inc.) Vol. 9, No. 1/2, 1999, pp. 67-72; and: *Contract Pastoral Care and Education: The Trend of the Future?* (ed: Larry VandeCreek) The Haworth Pastoral Press, an imprint of The Haworth Press, Inc., 1999, pp. 67-72. Single or multiple copies of this article are available for a fee from The Haworth Document Delivery Service [1-800-342-9678, 9:00 a.m. - 5:00 p.m. (EST). E-mail address: getinfo@haworthpressinc.com].

The fast-paced growth of Marketplace Ministries over the last 36 months continues through the 1998 year at a highly accelerated rate. The Ministry has nearly doubled in size since 1993 to its current state of nearly 200 companies and during the last two years has started with a new company every 15 days. They cover a vast geographical area, from Kansas to Texas, Pennsylvania to New York. Locations of the new client companies include Lebanon and Hatfield, Pennsylvania, as well as New York City, specifically Mt. Vernon, New York, just above Queens in New York City, Sioux City, Iowa, and several locations in Indiana.

Also, new companies were added in Dallas, Waco, and Austin, Texas; Greencastle, Pennsylvania; Grain Valley, Missouri; Overland Park and Olathe, Kansas. With these new workplace opportunities, Marketplace Ministries continues to draw interest from companies, both large and small, who desire to provide a chaplain-based Employee Assistance Program.

BOARD OF DIRECTORS

The first Marketplace Ministries' Board of Directors began in the summer of 1984, comprised mainly of friends of Mr. Stricklin and believers in him and this new ministry. Since then, the Marketplace Board has consisted of between 12 and 24 men and women who offer guidance and provide confirmation of the ministry's policy and procedures as well as voting on key issues.

The board usually meets two to three times a year at the National Headquarters in Dallas or at other special locations or retreats, as designated by the Executive Leadership Team. In recent years, the National Advisory Committee (NAC) has been established to provide additional oversight and wisdom. The NAC only meets once a year. The Marketplace Ministries' Foundation Board was formed in the spring of '98 and supervises this new ministry project.

The board members are expected to support the ministry through their work, prayer and financial gifts. Every board member is expected to make at least one work site visit each year with a Marketplace Ministries' Chaplain, as well as being a regular financial supporter of the ministry.

INTERFAITH COMMUNITY

MMI currently employs ministers from forty (40) different Protestant Christian denominations. We find the varied background of church polity and traditions adds significant depth to our teams of chaplains and makes them more accessible for ministry to individuals from different faith traditions. The chaplains also assist each other in understanding the perspectives brought to them by people in the client companies they are serving. Whenever we are together in a staff retreat setting we always have communion services together. This event is always a high point of our gathering as we unite around the Lord's Table for this special service.

The chaplains consider themselves extensions of the local churches into the business community. The chaplain's goal is to assist people with their life challenges in the context of biblical truth and Christian faith. They help individuals make professions of faith in Christ, and then assist them in finding a local Christian congregation of their choice in which to grow spiritually and serve the Lord, the church, and the community. Thus, the chaplains are co-workers with the local church ministers–never competitors.

All chaplains on our employed staff who serve in an assigned, back-up, or on-call role agree to and sign a statement of doctrinal beliefs established by the MMI Board of Directors.

We also have periodically employed Jewish and Catholic clergy in order to meet specific needs of individuals. On rare occasions, we have used the services of a clergyperson outside the Judeo-Christian tradition, such as a Buddhist monk, etc.

FUNDRAISING

The first funding to begin Marketplace Ministries came from Mr. Stricklin's personal funds. God graciously allowed money from his speaking engagements to come in to fund the new work along with Board of Directors' gifts and pledges.

From its opening year, Marketplace Ministries operates very differently than most Christian organizations. While the traditional model for most ministries is 80-20, meaning 80 percent of funding comes from donations from constituents and 20 percent comes from foundations, grants, wills, etc., Marketplace Ministries derives 90 percent of its income from client company contracts for whom it provides its Corporate Chaplaincy services. The remainder is from gifts, wills, and grants, etc. The ministry recently established a foundation with the stated goal of several million dollars to propitiate the continued and ongoing growth of this ministry.

GOVERNMENTAL AGENCIES

Marketplace Ministries has very limited contact with governmental agencies other than the normal functions of the IRS and state agencies. The Ministry has been granted 501-C3 tax-exempt status and is acceptable for tax-exempt giving. All of its income is subject to an annual audit and is in conformity with the guidelines of the nationally recognized Evangelical Council on Financial Accountability (ECFA).

PRODUCT IDENTITY AND MARKETING

Our product is pastoral care for people as a benefit of their employment. We do this through contractual agreements to provide a Corporate Chaplain program for corporations. The services of the Corporate Chaplain program include many of those provided by local church ministers to their congregations, e.g., hospital and home visitation, weddings, funerals, pastoral advice, Bible studies or devotionals, and crisis intervention. We also are present at the company site at least once per week to provide availability to the employees. Our program also covers the immediate family members of the client company employees.

We do not have an intensive marketing program. We gain prospects primarily through the recommendations of present clients who have found the chaplain service beneficial. Periodically, we receive an inquiry from a corporate leader who has seen publicity on our organization.

INTERNAL STRUCTURE

The chaplains who work for Marketplace Ministries are actual employees of the ministry rather than employees of the individual companies. The ministry pays each chaplain a wage from the monies generated by the client company contract. It also pays their workman's compensation insurance, mileage and expenses. They may also elect to participate in the ministry's cafeteria insurance and retirement plans.

While Marketplace Ministries has more than 500 Chaplains on its staff, the vast majority of its employees are part-time, mainly pastors and other ministry leaders who serve a few hours per week in individual companies in their home cities.

The ministry is structured so each person is held accountable. We have four regional managers, each responsible for a certain area of the country, nearly three dozen members of a nationwide leadership team, a full-time headquarters' staff, and the previously mentioned Board of Directors.

THE FUTURE

With God's rich blessings over the first 15 years, we are truly excited about the future at Marketplace Ministries. We pray for continued growth reaching into companies from California to the Carolinas with a caring, compassionate corporate chaplain who shows the love of Jesus.

Along with the previously discussed Marketplace Ministries Foundation, two of the most exciting Ministry programs for the future are the Mentoring Program and the Corporate Chaplaincy Degree Program.

Since mid-1997, Marketplace Ministries has attempted to share what we do and how we help individuals interested in replicating similar programs across the country. Our executive leadership has made a strong commitment to help others and not feel we have the exclusive franchise on this type of work. Typically, individuals will come to the National Headquarters in Dallas for a week of intensive training and hands-on experience along with possible travel to other cities or client sites for in-person training and experience. There is extensive follow-up when these persons return to their city, including referrals and on-call mentoring available at all times. We have designated one of our most senior members of the headquarters' staff to oversee this important process.

The Corporate Chaplaincy degree program was started at a single seminary in 1997 because there was limited training for individuals interested in doing this ministry. Currently, Marketplace Ministries provides a senior staff member who actually teaches the seminary classes on Corporate Chaplaincy. The seminary lists the classes in their academic catalogs, helps recruit the students and puts together a degree plan for the program. The ultimate success of this program, which includes an internship with Marketplace Ministries, will help overcome one of the biggest challenges facing us, namely finding qualified and trained chaplains. This seminary program has quickly doubled in size and our goal is to have 40 seminaries offering degrees in this vital ministry in the next five years.

GENERAL ADVICE

Looking back from the small and humble beginnings in 1984, it's truly amazing to see where this journey of faith has taken us. We daily seek to give God all the glory for any earthly success we have achieved along with learning the lessons, both positive and negative, we have experienced at Marketplace Ministries.

The best things we have done:

- Maintained a commitment to our original Mission Statement: Evangelism, Discipleship, and Christian service.
- Kept our personnel standards high to always provide exceptional chaplains and service to our client companies.
- Always operated on a cash basis–never borrowed money for anything.
- We seek to adequately orient and train new personnel.
- We carefully guard our relationships with client companies. Our client list is confidential and is not for sale or available for use by anyone. We

do not allow any other ministry or company to use our client relationships in order to gain an entree into our client companies.

- We seek to honor, express appreciation to, and reward all staff, especially the frontline chaplains who provide ministry for our clients.

The mistakes we have made:

- In the early days we did not always adequately train new personnel and we lost a limited number of client companies because of poor service. We underestimated the differences between local church ministry and corporate ministry.
- At one time our fees were based on the number of hours of ministry performed. Today our fee is established on the number of employees in each client company.
- There have been times we have broadened the services we offer in order to enhance our client relationships (seminars, personality testing, etc.). These additional services diverted us from fulfilling our original mission statement.

The Northern Rockies Clinical Pastoral Education Center, Inc., Billings, Montana

Richard A. Becker, MDiv
F. Alvin Embry, ThM

HISTORY AND DEVELOPMENT

A little over ten years ago the pastoral care directors at the two regional hospitals in Billings, Montana decided to collaborate in the creation of a renewed CPE program for Montana. A program at Deaconess Billings Clinic had provided extended units of CPE from 1982 until 1987 when the supervisor took a job in another state. The Deaconess Billings Clinic decided not to continue their CPE center and this left the region without a supervisor or center. The new pastoral care director at Deaconess Billings Clinic decided to initiate conversations with the director at Saint Vincent Hospital about the possibility of both hospitals developing a community-based CPE program.

A community-based CPE program? A freestanding CPE center in Montana? At first, neither director of pastoral care knew what this would look like. They did not even know if such a program existed. Yet each desired CPE to return to Montana. Each director desired interns to be placed in their hospitals. Each was willing to ask for funding. Each was naive enough not to know what they were getting into. And most importantly, each was willing to meet weekly at Billing's best Italian restaurant to plan this endeavor.

Rev. Richard A. Becker is Manager, Pastoral Care, Deaconess Billings Clinic. Rev. F. Alvin Embry is Executive Director, Northern Rockies CPE Center, Inc.

Address correspondence to the authors at: Northern Rockies CPE Center, Inc., P.O. Box 1164, Billings, MT 59103 (E-mail: alembry@mcn.net).

[Haworth co-indexing entry note]: "The Northern Rockies Clinical Pastoral Education Center, Inc., Billings, Montana." Becker, Richard A., and F. Alvin Embry. Co-published simultaneously in *Journal of Health Care Chaplaincy* (The Haworth Pastoral Press, an imprint of The Haworth Press, Inc.) Vol. 9, No. 1/2, 1999, pp. 73-79; and: *Contract Pastoral Care and Education: The Trend of the Future?* (ed: Larry VandeCreek) The Haworth Pastoral Press, an imprint of The Haworth Press, Inc., 1999, pp. 73-79. Single or multiple copies of this article are available for a fee from The Haworth Document Delivery Service [1-800-342-9678, 9:00 a.m. - 5:00 p.m. (EST). E-mail address: getinfo@haworthpressinc.com].

FUNDING

The first challenge was funding. How is a community-based CPE center to be funded? Inherent in this structure is the understanding that the community that is served by CPE is the source of its funding. The directors developed an optimistic annual budget proposal of $100,000 and asked their hospitals to fund half. The two hospitals would receive the greatest benefit of the program, thus it was felt they should provide a major part of its budget. The other half of the budget would hopefully come from churches and their judicatories, individual donations, grants, student tuition and fees from additional placement centers.

The administrators saw things from another vantage point. The hospitals were thankful that CPE could continue in Montana with neither organization being responsible for funding the program in its entirety. They saw a joint venture with each other and the community as a real opportunity to share costs. St. Vincent's, though they were incurring new costs, saw this as an opportunity to receive the benefit of interns and to contribute to pastoral education.

Both administrations agreed to provide $25,000 with the understanding that "matching funds" would be sought (sought but not required!). The directors were now ready to move beyond their weekly luncheons and seek the consultation of the Pacific Region of ACPE.

CONSULTATION

The Pacific Region of ACPE was contacted and updated concerning the desire of the Billing's hospitals to renew CPE in a community-based center. A site visit was planned for May 1988 with regional representatives.

Several meetings were planned. The first was with the pastoral care directors to update the site team on their progress. The second was with a group of interested community members, mostly clergy who were familiar with the CPE process. This was to mutually demonstrate the interest of the community clergy in CPE and the interest of the Pacific Region in Billings. This community group was also a precursor to developing an organizational task force and eventually a board of directors. The site team also met with the hospital administrators to acknowledge their support of the program. Finally a group of prospective students was invited to meet with the supervisors.

It was this last group that demonstrated most readily the need to restart CPE in Montana. About twenty persons, including both lay and clergy, attended to show their desire for CPE in Montana. The site team was reminded of Montana's geographic isolation. The closest CPE centers to Billings are hundreds of miles away in any direction.

The site team endorsed the plans and encouraged the developing task force to keep them informed as well as call on them for continued consultation. They were a little concerned about raising the second half of the budget from the "community" and maintaining the first half from the hospitals. Yet the thinking was that this, as well as other needs, would hopefully fall into place as time went on. Mostly, they were pleased with the enthusiasm that they encountered in all their meetings. They were also very much aware of the need to keep CPE in Montana.

ORGANIZATION

The money has now been raised, at least enough to provide a supervisor's salary. The enthusiasm was there. Potential students were calling weekly. A number of persons were willing to work on an organizational task force and the Pacific Region gave their blessing to proceed. So, how did this group proceed?

The directors chose about a dozen persons to join with them in developing the program. This group consisted of clergy with some CPE training or awareness; a couple of physicians who valued spiritual care; one interested layperson who was a person of considerable wealth, and an attorney who was invaluable in helping to incorporate the program. They met on a monthly basis and evolved from a task force to an incorporated board of directors.

The hospitals began to provide the funding after incorporation. These funds were important in that they provided savings on which to draw in the future. They also represented the financial viability of the program to potential supervisors.

THE SEARCH FOR A SUPERVISOR

The board was ready to recruit a supervisor who would also serve as the administrator of the program. They knew this could take some time. Many board members became uneasy about the lack of an administrator to help with the fund-raising and other details of the program. Also it seemed like things were not moving fast enough and some wanted to give legitimacy to the program by having such a person in place. They thought of hiring an administrative assistant. Instead, a friend of one of the board members was hired as administrator after much difficult discussion.

The administrator helped to organize board meetings, fund-raising, mailing lists, communications and office facilities. He was very energetic yet when supervisors were interviewed it became apparent that they did not see a need for such a position. They preferred a secretary or administrative assistant. Furthermore, the finances were prohibitive to keeping the administrator once the supervisor was hired. The administrator was let go immediately before the supervisor was hired.

The second issue that concerned supervisors was the financial stability. The promised $50,000 grants from the hospitals were seemingly not as secure as funding in-hospital-based CPE programs. Hospital-based programs, with funds that usually come directly out of pastoral care budgets, were at that time considered more secure. One supervisor indicated that he would be interested when we had $100,000 in our account. We knew we needed a supervisor with a little faith and an adventurous spirit.

The adventure of re-starting CPE in the wilderness of Montana proved to be an important attraction for a supervisor. Also, the board, willing to let go of their administrator, demonstrated to the interviewees that they were open to comprehensive leadership from the supervisor. Many supervisors liked the idea of reporting to a board with spiritual sensibilities. This seemed more attractive than reporting to a hospital administrator or, worse yet, a manager of social services.

The board received about five serious applications and ruled out two who were one step away from full supervisory certification. The remaining three interviewed well yet only one was willing to take the step of faith. Though funds were in place, the program needed more security. Though CPE had been present in Montana before, its center's accreditation had lapsed. Though the Pacific Region was enthused about the efforts to re-start and re-format a community-based CPE program, the supervisor and board had the hard work ahead of a new accreditation process. This was a major step of faith for any supervisor to take. The board was pleased that one supervisor was willing to leave the security of a well-established hospital-based center to come to Montana and a freestanding CPE program.

THE PROGRAM

The supervisor encountered such enthusiasm for training that he and the board determined to start a non-accredited CPE-like program for students who did not wish to wait for accreditation. The board also wondered just what the supervisor would do if he did not provide some sort of training during this time. Two such "units" were provided until the center received its accreditation. Once accredited, the supervisor was able to add a summer session and a satellite center in Great Falls to the extended Billings program.

Currently the program is under the direction of its second supervisor who conducts training in Billings, Great Falls and Bozeman, Montana. All of the satellite centers provide additional opportunities for students as well as funding for the program. Satellite centers are also being planned for other areas of

Montana. The board now wrestles with the problem of growth that comes with the fulfillment of the vision of two pastoral care directors who enjoy CPE and Italian cuisine!

ADVANTAGES OF THE FREESTANDING MODEL: THE SUPERVISOR'S PERSPECTIVE

There are a number of advantages in utilizing this model for Clinical Pastoral Education. Admittedly, some of these advantages may appear just the opposite to some, but from our perspective the gains far outweigh the costs. The principal advantage, in our view, is the tremendous amount of flexibility allowed by this model. For example, during the last 12 months, we have had students doing their clinical work in two separate, moderate-sized secondary care centers, a psychiatric center, a very small community hospital with an extended care facility, a parish, a hospice, etc. These students were not all in the same training group, nor was each student assigned to multiple training sites, but almost every training group will have multiple sites represented. This leads to cross-fertilization and sharing of resources and models. There is also an experiential realization that what works in Site A may not work so well in Site C.

Within this model, each site has a clinical facilitator whose role is to facilitate the student's integration into the facility. Wherever possible, we utilize the gifts and experience of a member of the Pastoral Services Department. This provides the student with an additional role model and an advocate. Students may also utilize the clinical facilitator as a consultant in their learning process. Optimally, the student will have a relationship with an experienced professional who has internalized and integrated the clinical method of learning and who has become his or her own supervisor.

Another advantage of this model is that it forces the student to take more responsibility for his or her own learning. The student must identify areas of learning that are unique to the clinical site and design (or discover) ways to maximize their learning. In the process of doing that and discussing it with the peer group, the benefit is shared. For example, in the intensive summer unit, we utilize the two hospitals in Billings. One of these facilities has obstetrics and pediatrics and the other doesn't. When the students from one facility start discussing their experiences in the neonatal nursery or the pediatric unit, the other students are stimulated to learn something about these areas also. Students are encouraged to identify resources and share them with the group. This summer, for example, one student who was working on a Rehabilitation unit discovered a particularly helpful neuropsychologist and asked her to do a presentation for the group. The group felt that she was so informative, they invited her to come back for a second presentation. This added a significant experience for the other students that they would not have gotten otherwise.

As a clinical pastoral educator, this model for doing CPE has forced me away from psychoanalytically-based supervision and into a more professional education-based supervisory style. The focus is on students as learners rather than on their interpersonal dynamics. A discussion of the relative merits of these two styles, indeed, philosophies, must be reserved for another time and place. As an educator, I feel responsible to send professionals-in-training to the clinical site. Students are required to bring clinically-based material to supervision rather than their own intra-personal struggles.

Another advantage of this model for me is that my students are more frequently adult learners in the truest sense of the word. Given the change in the demographics of most seminaries, this may not be unique to this setting. Because of the flexibility in programming offered by this model, students frequently come who are engaged in a more or less successful practice of their primary–or even secondary–profession. They frequently are in a discernment process, paying attention to what they feel may be a vocation. In this part of the country this is becoming more and more typical of those who do ministry. I think that these students are more serious about their learning and about their vocation. They are less resistant and more trusting of authority. It appears to me that they have much less trouble with the clinical method of learning than do younger, less experienced students.

Finally, and arguably most importantly, this model for doing CPE makes Clinical Pastoral Education available to students who probably would never have the opportunity to take it otherwise. Montana, though not densely populated, is a very large state. We become accessible by taking the resources of the center to the student, rather than insisting that every student come to the center. Many of our students are laypersons who are employed full time. They may be able to manage a few hours a week to participate in structured learning experiences, but not be able to add on lengthy travel time or participate in an intensive, full-time unit. This also makes it possible for sites that would not have any interest in becoming fully-accredited centers to experience having CPE students. This improves the amount of Spiritual Care available and often creates a broader, more realistic understanding of the role of spiritual care at the site.

The original vision for Northern Rockies Clinical Pastoral Education Center was to make Clinical Pastoral Education available to the entire state and region. We continue to hold that vision, continually seeking ways to reach underserved areas. The list of sites where CPE is or has been conducted continues to grow. In the past year we have added two sites in Montana and one in Northern Wyoming. We are currently attempting to secure funds to further develop this ministry by utilizing interactive television. Conversations are being held with the Regional Accrediting Commission and with a local interactive TV network. If successful in this effort, we will greatly expand our ability to reach students.

In some ways, the vision that motivated the development of this center has reached fruition. Yet there remain a number of areas in the state we have not touched. We continually seek ways to reach those in these areas. We are also beginning to look at other educational options to offer to the community. As more and more judicatories emphasize continuing education for their clergy, opportunities abound. There is also a growing dependence on lay pastoral care providers, who have little or no theological education, but are utilized to provide the bulk of the Pastoral Care in their congregation. We anticipate this movement will require the development of new paradigms.

Rocky Mountain Pastoral Care and Training Associates, Littleton, Colorado

Foy C. Richey, MDiv

HISTORY AND OVERVIEW

We formed the Rocky Mountain Pastoral Care and Training Associates, Inc. (RMPCTA) in 1994 when the Professional Concerns Committee of the Community Mental Health Institute-Ft. Logan, Colorado decided to move toward community-based CPE. This decision responded to requests from Pastoral Care Departments at Casper and Cheyenne, Wyoming that we bring community-based programs to their locations. The RMPCTA became a *satellite*[1] CPE promotional enterprise, the product of a new 501-C-3 not-for-profit agency.

As a satellite CPE operation, it was important that we form a vehicle that could reach beyond the statutory state boundaries in which our traditional hospital programs operated. With the support of hospital administration, we began conducting satellite CPE in Casper, Cheyenne, and, eventually Evanston, Wyoming as well as Scottsbluff, Nebraska and Anchorage, Alaska. Thus, RMPCTA's mission to provide CPE to new geographical areas and agencies was launched. The Colorado Springs Samaritan Counseling Center now conducts community-based CPE for RMPCTA and we have contracts pending with Farmington, New Mexico and Amarillo, Texas. We are explor-

---

Chaplain Foy C. Richey is President, Rocky Mountain Pastoral Care and Training Associates, P.O. Box 630, Littleton, CO 80160-0630.

Some of the ideas expressed here appeared in *The Satellite*, an occasional newsletter of the Rocky Mountain Pastoral Care Training Associates, Inc.

[Haworth co-indexing entry note]: "Rocky Mountain Pastoral Care and Training Associates, Littleton, Colorado." Richey, Foy C. Co-published simultaneously in *Journal of Health Care Chaplaincy* (The Haworth Pastoral Press, an imprint of The Haworth Press, Inc.) Vol. 9, No. 1/2, 1999, pp. 81-85; and: *Contract Pastoral Care and Education: The Trend of the Future?* (ed: Larry VandeCreek) The Haworth Pastoral Press, an imprint of The Haworth Press, Inc., 1999, pp. 81-85. Single or multiple copies of this article are available for a fee from The Haworth Document Delivery Service [1-800-342-9678, 9:00 a.m. - 5:00 p.m. (EST). E-mail address: getinfo@haworthpressinc.com].

ing opportunities in Las Vegas, Nevada and the Thornton Police Department (Colorado) as well as "prospecting" in Western Kansas for additional sites.

Pragmatically, we currently understand satellite CPE to be "contract CPE." This is similar to the "managed care" delivery of health and human services now popular in the national health care debate. Contract CPE follows in the current marketplace tradition of "outsourcing" services to institutions by less costly vendors. This is contractual in the strictest sense, in that the direct contract is with the student and institution and/or the student less the institution. Satellite/contract CPE, as we understand it presently, is less of a corporate structure and more of an inductive, community-based vending system where the education process is primary and the corporate structure is secondary. A community agency can sign one of two contracts: (1) a "Sponsor Contract" in which the agency (church, hospital, jail, etc.) contributes to program costs, or (2) a "Host Contract" in which agencies render only in-kind services, (i.e., meeting space, photocopy machine, phone, fax, etc.) without cash contribution. In this latter arrangement, the student tuition bears the brunt of the program costs.

The contract methodology is "Managed Care CPE." It is: (1) customer-friendly, (2) agency/short-term contract flexible,[2] and (3) inductive in its effort to tailor the curriculum to agency/geographical needs. This avoids the heavy administrative costs typically associated with an accredited center and a full-time employed supervisor. RMPCTA assumes the ACPE accreditation management responsibilities, which is, most of the time, a relief to the sponsoring or hosting agency that does not care to become ACPE accredited. The exceptions to this are also noteworthy; some agencies that wish to pursue ACPE accreditation can do so with specific contractual agreements as they continue to pursue the creation of more ongoing and extensive CPE programs.

Contrary to popular belief, satellite RMPCTA CPE has not been a lucrative moneymaking business thus far. Most of RMPCTA's income (90%) is paid directly to the training supervisors for their expenses. The ACPE assessment fees deplete the remainder. We have subsidized the financial losses of some satellites from the "earnings" of others in order to continue programs in those areas that cannot be self-supporting.

MARKETPLACE RECEPTIVENESS

Our initial efforts met with eager responses and further requests for programs. The South Central ACPE and National ACPE offices generously provided tuition grants. The "Wyoming project" as it was known, eventually expanded to Scottsbluff, Nebraska and various other agencies along the front range of the Rockies–Pueblo, Colorado Springs, Denver, and Greeley. The

Western Slope of the Rockies also took an interest, requesting separate programs in Grand Junction, Montrose[3] and Durango. In Denver, we earlier had contracted variously with Porter Memorial Hospital, Rose Medical Center, Lutheran Medical Center, West Pines Psychiatric Hospital, Boulder Community Hospital and the Denver Rescue Mission for satellite CPE programs. The Colorado Department of Corrections and the Colorado Division of Youth Corrections also utilized this satellite CPE programming.

We believe the clear and universal message of receptiveness is an expression of the usefulness of an agency "owning" a piece of its own tailored CPE program to fit its own indigenous needs. We see this receptiveness as the historically touted "inductive method" operating at its best.

This paradigm we variously termed "CPE PRN," "Outback CPE" and "Community-based CPE." But the central satellite-contractual (entrepreneurial) fiscal methodology has demonstrated its applicability and usefulness to a variety of marketplace contexts. Its flexibility to adapt and adjust the inductive method to the indigenous needs of the CPE customers is a big part of its success.

CONTRACTS

Contracts with sponsoring and/or hosting agencies vary in length and complexity. The CPE Student Handbook outlines the curriculum, but the agency contract includes all mutually agreed-upon safeguards for both parties, describing the parameters of desired interests. Professional guidelines for CPE quality assurance issues are built into the Student Handbook.

BUMPS AND GRINDS

There are incipient conflicts between the satellite marketplace methodology and the present ACPE corporate model. First and foremost, satellite CPE must often move quickly and precisely in order to gain a foothold on a market. The ACPE standards and accreditation procedures are bureaucratic and cumbersome by comparison.[4] They consistently mandate a "slow down" pace that can result in the loss of CPE customers. This serious deleterious effect of a major CPE accrediting agency prompts some satellite CPE programs to look at alternative CPE accrediting agencies for support and facilitation of satellite programs. These include the College of Pastoral Supervisors and Psychotherapists as well as the National Association of Catholic Chaplains.

This conflict is understandable. It is the same history of quarrel and conflict between all regulatory agencies and cutting edge creativity in the marketplace of goods and services. In a sense, theologically, it is a natural conflict between the "Kairos" or "right time" of marketplace CPE and the "Chronos," or "fullness of time" of the waiting period of the accreditation process necessitated by the CPE accrediting agencies.

In our experience, the inter-regional satellite marketing of CPE has met with substantially more resistance than the intra-regional marketing. The formal reason for this is that ACPE Standards must first guarantee quality assurance safeguards before programs can begin. The informal dynamic tends to reflect a "franchise boundary violation." While it is understood that the nine ACPE regions are not, in fact, "franchises," the regulatory ethos and function of the Standards do perform a curiously similar role. For example, the present ACPE Standards state that an inter-regional satellite operator "may" need to pay operational (assessment) fees in both regions (IX., E, 4., p. 31). Allegedly, these fees pay for potential grievance procedure costs; but so does marketplace franchise boundary-sharing pay for potential loss of market fees. Both are sharing in the liability costs of operating in a given market space.

We do not yet know whether corporate ACPE bureaucratic accreditation "slow down" methods will be challenged with grievances or appeals to antitrust or interstate commerce violations, but satellite CPE methodology and accordant marketplace timing raises the specter of such uncertain "futures."

FUTURES (AND "PORKBELLIES")

What does the future hold for satellite CPE. It's not all "pork bellies!" During the first three years of operation the RMPCTA books show essentially a "break even" budget. One CPE bureaucrat was recently overheard to state that this project is a "shipwreck waiting to happen!" We suspect that such a prediction may be more a function of one individual's wishful thinking than of reality. Rather, our present assessment is that satellite CPE is here to stay, if not in this present form then in some future format.

Will this marketplace methodology become more popular than the current highly subsidized hospital-based CPE funded systems? In the present managed health care market, it would seem so! Why wouldn't CEOs be interested in a lower cost contract to train their chaplains rather than a higher cost FTE/CPE residency program with a stipend?

This new development obviously introduces the prospect of increasing numbers of freestanding pastoral care corporations conducting CPE programs on a satellite basis. Geographic boundaries will likely be a relic of the past with air travel, E-mail and interactive television. The Veteran's Administration is already looking at interactive television by which to conduct CPE with geographically distant centers. One of our Wyoming CPE satellite programs is planning to use interactive television in a pilot project next year.

And what does E-mail offer the CPE process on the Internet? These are considerations yet unexplored and undiscovered in the electronic age. How can group process sensitivities be negotiated, for example, by using electronic media? One CPE colleague is personally conducting a two-year E-mail CPE supervision project with Japanese students. We anticipate satellite CPE to be a significant shaping and molding factor in the development of this electronic medium for future pastoral/spiritual care training. Marketplace cost effectiveness will mandate exploration of all alternatives within this venue.

This brief essay describes one model of satellite CPE; there are obviously many others. Presently I am told that there are twelve (12) ACPE centers in the U.S. conducting some form of "satellite CPE." We contend that not all of these efforts are "bona fide" satellite CPE. One large CPE center director calls his satellites "entrepreneurial" when he describes mini-CPE programs operating in various branches of his corporate health care system. We do not concur that such an operation is satellite-entrepreneurial. Rather, such an operation is a corporate health care subsidy of a branched-out system that is managed by a corporate pastoral care department head. This is subsidized corporate CPE; not satellite/contract/entrepreneurial.

CPE corporate structures are in jeopardy of reversing the time-honored, inductive method of learning in deference to a deductive or reductive methodology, superimposing a priori learning assumptions onto the human experience of valuing and creativity. It is yet to be seen whether a satellite model will offer a venue for recovering and retaining the central values of inductive methodology.

NOTES

1. This essay initially described "entrepreneurial CPE." Certain ACPE colleagues argued that it would be deleterious to RMPCTA to argue for entrepreneurial CPE at this time, given the changes within ACPE. Yielding to this argument, I have argued instead for "satellite" CPE.

2. Most contracts are designed for one to three years only with a review mandated at the end of this period. This provides opportunity for both the vendor (RMPCTA) and the recipient agencies to exit appropriately.

3. Jack Slaughter was actually the first "satellite CPE supervisor" with CMHI-Ft. Logan when he contracted (initially through the Presbyterian/St. Luke's Hospital of Denver, and later through Ft. Logan) to supervise a group of students (1992) at the Grand Junction Veteran's Administration Hospital.

4. This is true of most "voluntary efforts," i.e., How much we know about slowness of service delivery with voluntary chaplaincy?

RESPONSES TO: CONTRACT PASTORAL CARE AND EDUCATION: THE TREND OF THE FUTURE?

Response to Freestanding Clinical Pastoral Education Centers

William J. Baugh, DMin

The phenomenon of freestanding Clinical Pastoral Education (CPE) centers was a forward looking response by those who recognised the need for pastoral care and/or CPE when pastoral care had been deemed unworthy of adequate support from those within the institution. Inevitably the founder or initiator of the center was a person of faith or group committed to the provision of that service and who had the commitment, vision, and energy to start a risky, but promising venture.

The varied examples that have been selected for presentation here display a rich mixture of motivation and mission. I have asked myself many questions as I ponder the quilted landscape of freestanding centers. Is the relative-

Rev. William J. Baugh is Vice President of Religion and Health, Christ Hospital and Medical Center, Advocate, Oak Lawn, IL 60453.

[Haworth co-indexing entry note]: "Response to Freestanding Clinical Pastoral Education Centers." Baugh, William J. Co-published simultaneously in *Journal of Health Care Chaplaincy* (The Haworth Pastoral Press, an imprint of The Haworth Press, Inc.) Vol. 9, No. 1/2, 1999, pp. 87-91; and: *Contract Pastoral Care and Education: The Trend of the Future?* (ed: Larry VandeCreek) The Haworth Pastoral Press, an imprint of The Haworth Press, Inc., 1999, pp. 87-91. Single or multiple copies of this article are available for a fee from The Haworth Document Delivery Service [1-800-342-9678, 9:00 a.m. - 5:00 p.m. (EST). E-mail address: getinfo@haworthpressinc.com].

ly new presence or growth of these centers a sign of the health of CPE or the beginning of its demise? Is it a move that shows strength for the future or is it a holding action that comes as a by-product of the health care crisis in our country? Would I want to do it? How secure is it? Obviously, where funding is solid and deep that question is moot. But, the question remains in all of these circumstances, "Where are the owners, the vested stakeholders?" The original ownership seems to have largely rested in the vision of some creative individuals or groups. What has happened as the leadership has changed? "Does lack of ownership of the programs by hospitals or other sites signify a lack of investment in the provision of the service?" "Is it a sign of the atrophy of the significance of pastoral care and CPE?"

In this response I wish to assert that: (1) the primary allegiance of the chaplain or, indeed other employee is crucial; (2) that the missional influence on the organization can be significant when room is made for such influence; (3) that a prophetic stance is an important part of the role of pastoral care and; (4) that the provision of pastoral care most often comes before the proof of its value. Movement toward outsourcing may, in the end, be a missed opportunity for pastoral care to prove its worth.

Some freestanding centers are enormously successful and the envy of the CPE and pastoral care world. Of significant note is The HealthCare Chaplaincy, Inc. in New York City, the product of incredible marketing expertise, energy and ability to tap the philanthropy of the New York City area. The McFarland Institute in New Orleans is another successful model started as a foundation dedicated to the support of pastoral care and CPE with the proceeds of the sale of hospitals to a for-profit company. It established the place of pastoral care and education as separate and free from the immediate concerns of the marketplace when the for-profit organization entered the picture. This would not have happened without the vision and faith commitment of people at the center of the sale of the not-for-profit hospital.

Other freestanding centers have risen or fallen on the efforts of committed CPE supervisors. To be sure, the motive may have been a mixture of self-interest of the supervisor in staying in the area along their commitment to the future of CPE in that setting or area. I know well the enormous efforts of two talented women in Savannah, Georgia after their hospital-based CPE program was terminated. Jo Clare Wilson and Nancy McCormick spent 2 years trying to build a freestanding CPE center seeking CPE contracts with other institutions. Their efforts were courageous. Income was uncertain. Eventually, the need for more security won the day and appropriately so. They learned some valuable lessons. They had no external support as they started. It is important to have a nucleus of support, financial and otherwise, preferably from the church community before setting forth on the freestanding journey.

I remember many years ago when David Koch left the Eastern region of

ACPE to take a leap of faith in Toledo, Ohio. That effort and the ensuing contracts he was able to establish, lead to the successful, secure, and well-supported center, freestanding to be sure, that exists today.

As I read the presentations and wrestled with the questions I became more and more uncomfortable. I know virtually all of the people who built these creative pastoral care and CPE programs. The ministries they perform are full of depth and significance to so very many people. This was not just an ethereal exercise for me. It is the livelihood and commitment of friends. I began to think of these centers more dispassionately when I was able to see them as centers for the "outsourcing" of pastoral care. This is where I ran into difficulty, however. "Outsourcing" means giving up control, often ownership of the program. It means distance, loss of commitment to the central mission.

A recent increase in the focus on managed care, on for-profit health care, on downsizing, on outsourcing, and other cost-saving efforts has furthered the development and success of these centers. But the beginning and successful attempts to develop these centers came from people who saw the need. I suspect it most often started as a germ of an idea for one person who enlisted others and still others. At this point it meant either hiring a pastoral care specialist or teacher or forming a board. In all cases, it required talented people to carry on the vision and the task.

Let me speak from personal experience for a moment. I have worked for two faith-based hospitals in my career. The fact that they were faith-based was important to me. The tie to the mission motivated me. I had a strong sense of a higher purpose. I know that the not-for-profit secular hospital's mission of caring is crucial for all employees and especially chaplains. What is that sense of mission, of buying into a common vision like for the "outsourced" chaplain? I found myself pondering those differences? What is it like to work at one institution and be paid by a different organization?

As I wrote this response I became aware that I had an "outsourcing" experience in my history though we didn't call it that then. Before entering the ministry, I was a food service director for a national company. The schools and colleges were our customers. They "outsourced" their food services to us. We lived in the culture of the outsourced. We were guests of the institution. We were tangential to their primary mission of education. In contrast, the food service operation in the hospital where I work now seems much more related to the central mission of the hospital than I did back then.

As I write this, the system I work for is exploring the option of outsourcing its pharmacy services. Obviously, that is a crucial service in a hospital and does not signify a decrease in importance. However, I understand that the success of these attempts to outsource pharmacy services across the country have not been well received. The "outsourced" pharmacists do not have the commitment and allegiance to the central mission of the hospital in which they work. In the same way, do the "outsourced chaplains feel disconnected from the primary mission of the hospital or other setting in which they spend their time? To be sure, some have been in their setting for many years. Is there a difference in commitment? In the sense of belonging?

Yet, is there not an essential difference when one considers pastoral care services? The need for those services is less well defined and recognized than pharmacy services or food services. We in pastoral care are in a situation where the initial provision of pastoral care services can, and often does, lead to its further development. But pastoral care must prove its value through relationships and through service. In other words, the provision of the service can prove its value and lead to success. Often, its value is not recognized when the service is not seen as personally important to the decision-maker or no convincing data exists to prove that value. Pastoral care and Clinical Pastoral Education were able to prove their value because someone first believed in it and then, it proved its worth to the institution.

For example, in the setting where I presently serve, pastoral care services were initiated by a forward-looking, visionary, and committed chief executive. The service was provided and chaplains began playing a crucial part in the health care team. As in the popular movie, *Field of Dreams*, "It was built and they came." Just as I am writing this now our on call chaplain stopped in and spoke about how busy this Saturday morning has been–15 codes in 5 hours.

But the Department of Religion and Health is more than patient care services at Christ Hospital and Medical Center. And it seems to me that is a crucial difference from secular and "outsourced" pastoral care. Religion and Health has missional influence at the highest levels of the system. I would argue that this influence could not be sustained with "outsourced" pastoral care. An "outsourced" pastoral care function would not have the acceptance and the integration into the fabric of the management and mission of the organization at every level.

To be sure, one might argue that most of these freestanding centers do not operate in a church-sponsored environment like Christ Hospital. It could be posited that the secular institution is less driven by a central mission, making integrated chaplains less important. That is not at all clear to me. The mission of not-for-profit health care institutions have a focus on caring and healing that is every bit as much of a motivator as in a denominational hospital. Ken Blanchard, author of the *One Minute Manager*, says "Those committed to the mission, purpose, and values of the organization will work together like squirrels gathering their food."

And then one must ask the question we chaplains sometimes fail to ask in the institutional setting, "What place the prophetic?" Obviously, there is never a comfortable place for the prophet, especially if security is a high need. But, I would argue that the prophet is in a better place to have his or her prophecy heard if the hearer knows that the prophet has a stake in the outcome, cares about the future of the institution and feels an ownership of the resources, both personnel and material.

Are these stories of the beginnings of freestanding centers similar to stories of the prophets and missionaries of old fighting the odds and striking out in faith to carry on a mission and fight the powers of resistance? Well, I would not want to make an excessive claim as we look at the big picture. I would, however, conclude by asserting that the question of primary allegiance is crucial.

I would also suggest that in some sense all of us who are in ministry are, indeed, "outsourced." Most of our faith groups understand their deployment of clergy as a type of outsourcing. As a Methodist minister I know what outsourcing is. We are ordained to the Annual Conference. In a sense we are all outsourced to the churches and many are in specialized ministry. But we are all under the appointment of a bishop and serve at his or her pleasure. Our primary allegiance is to the mission of the wider church and the Annual Conference of brother and sister ministers. That is comforting, motivating and certainly adds to my sense of carrying on a mission together, a mission that does not stop at the local church level. Is that not true of the understanding for rabbis, the Catholic Church, Episcopal, etc.

So, is there value in freestanding pastoral care centers? Of course, for if the ministry to persons in great need is to happen, it is because of the vision of people who see that need and are committed to easing that need. Our mission and mandate comes from beyond the institution. It comes from a higher source. For those of us who call ourselves Christian, the mandate is to speak of the message of love for all people. With that lofty mission, "outsourcing" becomes a management philosophy, not a missional imperative.

Responses to the "Freestanding Stories"

Larry Burton, ThD

During the past several months I have received at least one call per week asking for advice about how to avoid being downsized or what to do if one is downsized. One of these callers asked, "Do you think we ought to form one of those freestanding chaplaincy things? I hear they are the coming thing."

Whether or not freestanding chaplaincy organizations are the "coming thing" is open to debate. However, this volume of stories testifies that there are a variety of successful models. Most of us professional chaplains have spent much–if not all–of our careers in health care organizations that hire us, pay us, and from which we hope eventually to retire. I am personally only one generation away from the man I believe to have been the first "professional" hospital chaplain. My mentor, Chaplain Les Potter, spent forty years faithfully serving a single institution. My callers, on the other hand, are worried that they will not have this opportunity. I have a couple of responses to this concern.

First, the world of health care has indeed changed in recent years and some chaplains have been downsized. Such administrative decisions have caused pain for the chaplains and reduced the overall quality of care for patients–at least that is my observation. Second, as I pointed out above, it was barely more than a half-century ago that health care organizations had professional chaplains at all! I simply do not believe that professional chaplaincy is under siege any more than I believe that freestanding chaplaincy organizations are the wave of the future. Institution-based and freestanding chaplaincy services are examples of the old aphorism "There's more than one way to skin a cat."

"Where your gifts and the world's need intersect, there is your call," my

---

Larry Burton is affiliated with the Department of Religion, Health and Human Values, Rush-Presbyterian-St. Luke's Medical Center, Chicago, IL.

[Haworth co-indexing entry note]: "Responses to the 'Freestanding Stories.'" Burton, Larry. Co-published simultaneously in *Journal of Health Care Chaplaincy* (The Haworth Pastoral Press, an imprint of The Haworth Press, Inc.) Vol. 9, No. 1/2, 1999, pp. 93-96; and: *Contract Pastoral Care and Education: The Trend of the Future?* (ed: Larry VandeCreek) The Haworth Pastoral Press, an imprint of The Haworth Press, Inc., 1999, pp. 93-96. Single or multiple copies of this article are available for a fee from The Haworth Document Delivery Service [1-800-342-9678, 9:00 a.m. - 5:00 p.m. (EST). E-mail address: getinfo@haworthpressinc.com].

father advised me as a young man. Ministering people have always responded to such advice. Long before there were professional chaplains, clergy persons of all faiths were bringing comfort to the sick and hope to the dying. In the midst of the 19th century, an Episcopal parish founded a small hospital–now a part of our large, academic medical center–at which the Rector "made daily rounds."[1] The publication of a recent study by Harold Koenig[2] in which a positive relationship between church attendance and shorter length-of-stay was demonstrated has prompted some of my colleagues to worry that administrators will interpret this as reason to return to the "daily rounds" of local clergy. I don't think so. Not only has the professional chaplain shown him or herself to be a vital and integral part of health care, the role of spirituality in health and healing is receiving increasing attention in scientific and administrative journals.

The question for me is this: is there a *best* delivery model for chaplaincy services and if so, what are the characteristics of that model.

The journey from local, autonomous delivery of pastoral care services, to institution-based departments of pastoral care (and education) to local, contract providers of pastoral care seems to me to be extremely short. Each is an expression of ministry in which (a) an "entrepreneur" recognizes a need and organizes a structure to support services to meet that need, (b) services are provided, (c) the providers of service are paid, and (d) there is accountability. The primary differences among the organizations have to do with their structure: local congregation-based, health care institution-based, or freestanding.

While the first issue raised by many of my callers is security (the second is a concern about patient care), it appears to me that–in the initial stages at least–chaplaincy cared little about security. They, as my grandmother was fond of observing, "stepped out in faith." The stories contained in this volume reflect a faith-filled vision as the genesis of the enterprise. Identifying a need is important, but articulating a vision to meet that need is even more important. Fr. Gene Sitzmann's advice to "think wild" is one example of the various approaches to articulating a vision. It appears that when the visionary is theologically grounded, the wild thinking can more easily take wing. At least that is my sense from reading the testimony of Dr. Ron Sunderland.

Articulating vision and bringing that vision into being require different skills. Common among the stories of chaplaincy pioneers is a powerful combination of vision, organizational ability, and fiscal savvy. Specialists in organizational development[3] describe the features of entrepreneurial leadership as being present at the beginning of most organizations with a new "product." While the needs may shift later in the "life cycle" it is pretty clear that this sense of vision, marketing, organization and fiscal savvy is central to initial success. This is tireless work, too. Constant marketing of the vision to congregations, community organizations, foundations, health care institutions, and individual donors is the order of the day. Add to that some ability in mergers and acquisitions (see the story of The HealthCare Chaplaincy, Inc.) as well as sales, and one has a picture of the unique personality needed to drive a new chaplaincy entity. To some extent, these qualities are needed whether the entity is freestanding or a part of a larger organization.

Not all of us in chaplaincy are equipped with these gifts. Many–if not most–of us are far better at laboring in the vineyard. (Perhaps that is why so many of us prefer the apparent security of working in the context of an existing health care institution, where our preference for one-on-one ministry seems to fit so well.) Some other "gifts differing," to borrow a phrase from Isabel Briggs Myers,[4] have to do with how we prefer to express both our autonomy and connectedness, and how we prefer to relate to authority.

Some of my colleagues have wondered if we ought not to encourage the creation of more freestanding chaplaincy service organizations. "That way, we will be in control, rather than health care administrators," commented one of my friends. Since I believe that there is more pure chaos in the economic–and therefore the health care–system, the idea that any one of us is actually "in control" is doubtful, and the creation of organizations with the goal of gaining some sort of control over this chaos is unlikely to prove helpful. On the other hand, where there is a need that is going unmet, and where existing institutions seem unable or unwilling to meet the need themselves, there is a future waiting to be born. Rural areas where clergy and laity yearn for training opportunities, underserved areas where needs exist but services do not–such as urban outpatients–or, areas where services are shifting because of outsourcing or downsizing: these are likely places for the emergence of freestanding chaplaincy organizations.

And what of the traditional, institution-based chaplaincy services? They will endure, but they will require vision, marketing and fiscal skills to continue their success. So are these freestanding, contract organizations a trend for the future? I don't think so. They are a manifestation of the visionary, ingenious, entrepreneurial spirit of creativity that has characterized ministry from the beginning. They are one-among-many responses to the direction, "where the world's need and your gifts intersect, there is your call."

Some final observations:

- The concern for security, while understandable, needs to find its response in terms of theology rather than economics.
- Chaplains have different gifts, and there is no one "right" structure for our work.
- Any organizational expression of chaplaincy ought to ground itself in the certification/accreditation standards of the profession (such as the Association of Professional Chaplains, The National Association of Catholic Chaplains, or the Association for Clinical Pastoral Education).

REFERENCES

1. J. Bowman. *Good Medicine*. Chicago: Chicago Review Press, 1987.

2. Harold Koenig & David Larson. Use of hospital services, religious attendance, and religious affiliation. *Southern Medical Journal*, 91(10), 1998, 925-932.

3. See W. Bridges, *The Character of Organizations*. Palo Alto: Consulting Psychologists Press, Inc, 1992 as well as R. Daft, *Organization Theory and Design*. Cincinnati: South-Western College Publishing, 1998, 173ff.

4. I.B. Myers with P.B. Myers. *Gifts Differing*. Palo Alto: Davies-Black Publishing, 1995.

Clinical Pastoral Education: Coming of Age

Al Lumpkin, STM

Serving on the Association of Clinical Pastoral Education's (ACPE) Standards Committee wasn't anything like what I had expected. Instead of rigidity and contentiousness, I experienced a sense of community, of rich collegiality. Moments of dialogue, and sometimes sharp debate, centered on core issues. I count the past six years working on Standards among the most powerful learning experiences of my professional life. Serving as secretary, keeping track of subtle wording changes sometimes kept me out of trouble, and the leadership of Mike Carlson and John Peterson challenged me to consider becoming chair. I don't intend that these thoughts represent any consensus of the Standards Committee, and I certainly don't speak for the ACPE. These are, rather, my impressions, which have grown stronger over the past several years and come into focus as my response to the nine stories found earlier in this volume.

Yesterday I read e-mail from a colleague that raised sharp and difficult questions. This morning, in the middle of this final draft, another peer called. I'm heartened by this kind of dialogue. More than that, I find myself reflecting on how being a clinical educator is far more than a career for many in the CPE community. I'd been trying to determine what kind of article this had become, and I suddenly sensed that it's an editorial about a deeper question I hadn't quite put into words. *Will this movement endure deeply into the twenty-first century?* In a rather startling way, CPE created its place in the 20th century wedged between two powerful forces, the religious communi-

Al Lumpkin is ACPE Supervisor, Geisinger Medical Center, North Academy Avenue, Danville, PA 17822.

[Haworth co-indexing entry note]: "Clinical Pastoral Education: Coming of Age." Lumpkin, Al. Co-published simultaneously in *Journal of Health Care Chaplaincy* (The Haworth Pastoral Press, an imprint of The Haworth Press, Inc.) Vol. 9, No. 1/2, 1999, pp. 97-104; and: *Contract Pastoral Care and Education: The Trend of the Future?* (ed: Larry VandeCreek) The Haworth Pastoral Press, an imprint of The Haworth Press, Inc., 1999, pp. 97-104. Single or multiple copies of this article are available for a fee from The Haworth Document Delivery Service [1-800-342-9678, 9:00 a.m. - 5:00 p.m. (EST). E-mail address: getinfo@haworthpressinc.com].

ties and American health care. This movement thrived because it met powerful educational and spiritual needs. So again, the question is whether this unique theological method can connect us around real needs, so that CPE will continue to thrive.

THE STRUGGLE OF CREATIVITY AND ACCOUNTABILITY

There is tension between the winds of spontaneous change, the creativity that seems to flow naturally from process education, and the need for clinical educators to be responsible to our students, the institutions and settings in which they minister, and the religious communities we serve. ACPE people place high value on autonomy, especially as it craves freedom to explore and discover new ways. The abiding purpose of the CPE movement is to provide for pastoral formation and learning that will lead the learner toward effective practice of ministry that is marked by integrity and competence.

The history of the CPE movement charts a unique course in theological education in which the student not only learns about ministry, but learns "into" the art form we call pastoral caregiving. It has demanded a price, namely that students risk the stripping away of personal, protective mechanisms in order to engage reality at its more painful places. CPE has consistently been about engagement and encounter, with the expectation that the learner will be changed. As s/he discovers truth in human turmoil and suffering, there emerges, even more importantly, truth about him or herself.

Clinical Pastoral Education grew with its bold claim that the student could be transformed. It has been our assumption that the minister's person is the primary tool of her/his ministry. CPE provided a setting in which basic assumptions were challenged precisely when pain could not be so easily evaded. The CPE movement championed the person's learning to face chaos and to participate in "universal human melancholia" as Henri Nouwen once said in a presentation. In the clinic, students encountered the potential to offer care and be "gotten to" by others. They also experienced the disappointing limits to their ability to offer hope and healing. Stories about "Summer CPE" are still carried back to the seminary, and it's not uncommon for someone to declare that s/he learned more in those twelve weeks than in previous years of formal education.

CPE's coming of age also has brought growing awareness of the importance of accountability. A learning process as powerful as this experiential method, which risks the stripping away of human defenses, can be redemptive or destructive. One person may experience transformation, while another is scarred. We reached growing awareness of the need for caution over the past decade; for example, we've discovered how many persons entering ministry have come out of experiences of abuse. The role of the supervisor and the engagement of a peer group are powerful resources. The other track of our history, and certainly a less celebrated development, has been the increasing consciousness of the need for accountability, including a core of ethical principle, policies that will protect student rights, and educational structure sufficient to "free up" and empower the CPE student to learn.

THE GIFT OF CHANGE

The educational method that underlies CPE evolved its way into a central role in two very different communities, somehow connecting with health care's need for "expressive" caregiving and the faith communities' need to prepare its practitioners to minister within profound human dilemmas. This movement has a colorful history, marked with persons of distinctive and strong conviction. The changes, forged both in its powerful alliances and sharp differences, has kept CPE alive. A somewhat different tension arises as the ACPE comes of age. We've moved into a maturity which, at once, makes our craft more effective *and* threatens to compromise its edge or stagnate its forms. The hopeful fact is that this "clinical method" and "process education" continues to draw persons who are willing to challenge complacency and risk change.

In the more recent years since the 1967 merger, CPE has experienced more change than we may immediately recall. Many of us remember when a CPE "quarter" meant precisely that, three months of full-time immersion in a clinical setting. I'm not certain who first entertained the idea of "extended" CPE, the part-time program designed as continuing education for parish clergy, but it met with suspicion and resistance. Would we, without this intensity, lose the very resource that created CPE's powerful learning? Extended programs are not the same, but they worked and, in fact, provided a point of entry into CPE for many of us who moved through residencies and into supervisory roles.

From its origins in mental and medical hospitals, CPE found its way into different settings precisely because of the clear understanding that these programs never were primarily about "hospital training." CPE was always an educational method for ministry formation; therefore, it could be carried out in a variety of settings–prison, geriatric facility, or parish. There have been ventures in community-based programs where chaplaincy students ministered in homeless shelters. Alliances with fire and police agencies called CPE students to scenes of crisis. Experiences of community settings pushed the ACPE, where the focus had been almost exclusively on the one-to-one pastoral encounter, to pay attention to how systems affect persons and ministry itself.

The evolution of *ACPE Standards* records subtle and important shifts in forms ACPE Centers have taken. Rather quickly, we've developed new procedures to accredit systems where CPE programs are administered centrally, with shared policies and procedures. The *1999 ACPE Standards* specifically recognizes freestanding centers, programs that develop agreements or contracts to provide ministry in a variety of settings.

Similar changes are occurring in Supervisory CPE, the result of pressures from at least two directions. First, educational consortia were created throughout the nine regions as supervisors recognized the importance of collaboration and consultation in the often daunting task of preparing Candidates to meet certification committees. Said differently, we've learned how difficult it is to provide adequate supervisory education without these collegial resources. Requirements for a supervisory peer group were removed some years ago, but with the understanding that the Supervisory Candidate is responsible to develop peership for her or himself on an ongoing basis.

The second influence on Supervisory CPE has been more dramatic. As financial resources became more scarce, institutions learned that Supervisory CPE is our most costly program. Educational demands on supervisory students often prevent them from providing much direct patient care. When Supervisory CPE is done well, it consumes much time from a training supervisor. Currently, many who are ready to enter the "certification track" are chaplains in their own institutions, persons who have seasoned and sharpened their clinical skills over several years of professional experience. These folks don't wish to leave established positions, and most couldn't afford life on a stipend. The answer seems to be the creation of contracted relationships between ACPE Centers accredited for Supervisory CPE and institutional settings where the potential candidate is already employed, where his or her supervision of students must take place. These arrangements are doubly creative. They foster the development of new ACPE Centers. It seems important for us to continue working at issues of accountability as we adapt our educational process to this rapidly changing scene.

The ACPE convened what we called the "ACTS Task Force" in 1994 to identify new directions. The resulting mandate to the Standards Committee was to clarify and simplify a document which, while filled with important information, was cumbersome and confusing. The text of the *1995 Standards* consumed 62 pages of policies, procedures, guidelines, sanctions, definitions, and benchmarks. The Standards Committee was asked to identify essential elements and principles of CPE and edit out the rest, which would be revised and published in the manuals of the respective commissions. In way of contrast, the text of the *1999 Standards* is 15 pages.

The intent of this project, which may not yet be very well understood, was to pave the way for change. This change makes sense, for at least four reasons: (1) This is more a more flexible and open structure. It is currently easier and quicker to make changes in response to emerging needs and possibilities–to accommodate innovation. (2) Policy and procedure matters are conceived and drafted by the commission members, who are the persons with greatest awareness of problems. These representatives, elected for the most part by the membership at the regional level, have the most experience in these respective areas. (3) There is an effective system of checks and balances. Changes in each of the manuals are reviewed by the Standards Committee to determine compliance with the intent of *ACPE Standards*. The manuals are then reviewed and approved by the Board of Representatives, which is responsible to represent the interests and concerns of the ACPE membership. (4) The ability of the membership to effect change is more pronounced than most people realize, but only as individuals pay attention to the changes and take the time to express their convictions. The purpose of the ACTS Task Force was not to inhibit anyone's practice of supervision, but to embrace creativity and vital change in the CPE movement.

WHAT'S ESSENTIAL?

I prepared to write this article by reading through the *1999 ACPE Standards* one more time. What stood out for me were historic components of this educational process so deeply ingrained that the loss of any one would change the essence of CPE. I came away with a renewed sense that, amid all the turmoil of the past two decades, we've managed to hold on to the core values of this movement. Six concepts stood out for me.

The *clinical method of learning* might be understood in several ways. CPE has always been an inductive educational design where the learning arises out of a student's experience. At the simplest level, he or she learns from what works and, sometimes even more powerfully, from what does not! The clinical design has been described as "affective" education, empowered by the felt need to know or understand something that is necessary for the ministry event that lies before the student today (or one that occurred yesterday). At a deeper level, the clinical method aims at the student's discovering new awareness or insight that will eventually be integrated within the person him/herself.

Without the *practice of ministry* CPE would become a pedantic form of observation or skill development. We've sometimes claimed that the patient (or her/his family members), client, or parishioner *is* the primary teacher. From the first day of the initial CPE Unit, the student is more than an observer. S/he is invited to participate in the creation of ministry. This venture into pastoral functioning may be the only way to learn "presence"–the power of empathic understanding and the efficacy of focused listening. Doing ministry, one develops awareness of important themes embedded in the story the person is trying to convey (and, with supervision, it may combat the short attention span that so often gets in the way). In any case, as the CPE student experiences the universal human needs of persons–needs to matter and to be understood–these ministry events teach her or him about the relational art of caregiving.

CPE's *process model of learning* is the reflective side of this inductive, or "action-reflection," educational design. The core of its curriculum is the engagement and dialogue that fosters discovery. The structure includes critique, elements of objective assessment from supervisor and peers, and development of the ability for candid self-evaluation. CPE aims for what Piaget calls "accommodative learning," which occurs when a student is faced with a piece of reality she or he can't fit into some familiar "big picture," and something must change. The ultimate objective is to equip students to superintend their own professional functioning.

The *peer group* structure of CPE makes it potentially much more powerful than an apprenticeship. The group is important for several reasons. The rabbi, priest, minister, or imam will encounter and work with groups throughout her or his professional life. Crazy things happen to people in groups. Joan Hemenway's book, *Inside the Circle* (published by Journal of Pastoral Care Publications, Inc., 1996), identifies how engagement within a group affects the student and how it affects his or her colleagues. Clearly the ability to function in groups is a core competency for clergy. In CPE, students learn about groups by becoming a group. The power of group learning in this process education is equally clear. In receiving and offering critique, the student learns how to learn. How else will a person develop the skill to build relationships with parishioners who are very different from her or himself? Our society, including the church, offers few opportunities for ministers to see themselves through the eyes and honest responses of others.

Competent *supervision* is obviously one of the elements. I recall someone saying that every group needs a supervisor, which started a fascinating discussion. It isn't that the supervisor necessarily knows better or more. Rather, in a peer learning group, the presence of the supervisor causes something different to happen–something different, for example, from the casual discussion in an institution's dining hall. The supervisor is responsible to keep focus on the process and help reveal or uncover deeper currents. Beyond this facilitation of the group, the supervisor provides competent critique. S/he works at creating and utilizing relational alliances with students individually. In a word, the supervisor's task is to create and maintain a setting in which interpersonal engagement and, hopefully, dialogue can occur.

The *individual contract for learning* keeps CPE from becoming a "one size fits all" method of advanced skill building. The *1999 Standards* identifies this contract as a collaborative effort of the student and supervisor. While "teachable moments" that create the most powerful learning are serendipitous, the student's effort to identify the gaps and deficits in her/his competency create an important focus for the educational process. Again, the supervisor-student alliance both creates and grows out of the contract for learning. Ultimately this inductive, clinical, process education is driven by the student's needs and motivation. The CPE supervisor becomes one of the key resources the student will utilize for his or her movement toward competence.

These six vital components are embedded in our history. They combine to create CPE's unique method of theological education; they create an identity we must not lose.

COMPETENCY AND OUTCOMES

The mission of CPE is to enable and enhance students' professional competency for ministry. We've struggled and experienced much difficulty in defining very clearly what this competency involves. The dilemma is, at least in part, the bewilderingly broad and extensive list of skills the professional clergy person must develop in one way or another. Another factor is the resistance of many pastoral educators to shift this inductive, process model, which has served CPE so well, toward a greater emphasis on content and, perhaps, shades of regimentation.

Over the past three years, the ACPE has faced its own accreditation review by the U.S. Department of Education (USDE), and we've been pushed to identify the outcomes of CPE programs. A friend who is a college physics professor said to me the night before the deadline for this article that we're all caught in a strong current of outcome-based education. The more I've become involved in the effort to fulfill USDE guidelines, the more my conviction has grown that meeting these requirements may involve surprisingly little change to our process. The USDE *is* pushing us to become more clear about how we function and to find ways to assess how well we're producing the learning and growth that our students sign on to achieve.

It seems important to say what the "outcomes" are. ACPE's first example appears in the *1999 ACPE Standards* section on "Introductory CPE." The seven listed outcomes represent an attempt to describe what a motivated student, with reasonable potential to become a successful minister, will accomplish in an initial 400-hour clinical program.

The language is carefully crafted to talk about students *meeting* these outcomes–not completing or fulfilling them. Outcomes are the "fields" of professional development a minister will address over and again at increasingly deep levels. These competencies consume one's professional lifetime. A student *meets* one of these objectives when s/he enters that field and begins to work at the task or ability. When a supervisor attests that a student has met any of these objectives, s/he is saying that the person has *entered* that arena and demonstrated engagement of the competency defined in the outcome.

An understanding of what these outcomes are *not* may also be important. The seven are not intended to circumscribe what will or should happen in the student's initial CPE Unit, as though this process could ever be reduced to a "one size fits all" procedure. Outcomes will not identify the core of the student's experience. It will not organize the curriculum or predict how or when teachable moments will happen. It is the collaboration of student and supervisor in creating a viable alliance and contract for learning that sets the stage for learning. The experience of ministry creates the grist. The quality of critique and dialogue in the peer group becomes the crucible from which affective learning emerges.

What the outcomes provide for the CPE process may be more valuable than we expect. They should create some clarity about otherwise hidden expectations, enhancing, rather than inhibiting, a student's freedom to explore pastoral functioning. For the one who is required to endure a CPE Unit, whose resistance tends to overcome his or her motivation, accountability attached to these outcomes may provide some helpful anxiety (and the awareness that it is possible to fail if one tries hard enough). Outcomes may be a valuable resource to help CPE students reach a realistic assessment of what needs to change and grow within themselves. Finally, these outcomes may provide perspective for demonstrating the viability and effectiveness of a new design or approach to clinical learning.

CONCLUSION

Will ACPE endure long into the twenty-first century? I still don't know the answer to this question. I'm not even certain that the question is ours to answer. However, it does seem important that we continue to identify the core values that have caused this movement to thrive, that we remain open to creativity and emerging possibilities, and that we embrace the need to be accountable for what we create. The increasing development of freestanding pastoral care and education centers presents interesting and important challenges around the issues of Standards. These organizations also struggle with creativity and accountability. They provide ACPE the gift of change and the possibility of vital dialogue within the Regions and the national leadership structures. We must welcome these opportunities.

Reflections on *Contract Pastoral Care and Education: The Trend of the Future?*

Frank S. Moyer, MDiv, BCC

The energy and faith-inspired creativity reflected in the stories of these organizations are, in themselves, gifts to the reader. Whether the impetus for new approaches was "reactive" or "proactive," all of them reflect commitment to bringing pastoral care and education to the communities they serve. Hopefully, the professional organizations in these fields will recognize the importance of those qualities as they seek ways to integrate these new approaches.

The Pastoral Care/Education "movement" is also indebted to Larry VandeCreek for the development of this volume. The approaches of these men and women need to be told, read, and critiqued both within the "movement" as well as outside. This is only possible when the ideas get transferred to written documents and reviewed in wider arenas.

I am also thankful for the opportunity to reflect and comment on these stories. Each story generated ideas and thoughts. Rather than simply present those in random fashion, my approach will be to focus them under certain questions with concluding comments at the end.

ARE "FREESTANDING" APPROACHES A NEW TREND?

The temptation is to answer "no" and "yes." The Lutheran Chaplaincy Service dates back to 1914 and The HealthCare Chaplaincy has existed since

---

Rev. Frank S. Moyer is a member of Professional Pastoral Resources, 995 North Main Street, Rockford IL 61103.

[Haworth co-indexing entry note]: "Reflections on *Contract Pastoral Care and Education: The Trend of the Future*?" Moyer, Frank S. Co-published simultaneously in *Journal of Health Care Chaplaincy* (The Haworth Pastoral Press, an imprint of The Haworth Press, Inc.) Vol. 9, No. 1/2, 1999, pp. 105-108; and: *Contract Pastoral Care and Education: The Trend of the Future?* (ed: Larry VandeCreek) The Haworth Pastoral Press, an imprint of The Haworth Press, Inc., 1999, pp. 105-108. Single or multiple copies of this article are available for a fee from The Haworth Document Delivery Service [1-800-342-9678, 9:00 a.m. - 5:00 p.m. (EST). E-mail address: getinfo@haworthpressinc.com].

1961. Others are in their second decade. Indeed, the approach of the Lutheran organization was very common prior to the 1960s. Many denominational groups, singly or in cooperation with others, sponsored pastoral care programs in a variety of facilities serving humans in need. Thus the "no" answer.

However, both the "old" and the "new" do reflect significant changes in their patterns of operation. These changes include funding mechanisms. Once almost solely obtained from denominational judicatories and/or local congregations, it is now principally sought through independent contracts with the institutions. The product has also changed. Once largely a "mission" ministry, now there is a strong emphasis on "professional services." Providers were once clergy selected from a pool of older, semi-retired, or persons with an evangelical zeal; today they are often "certified" chaplains and "accredited" centers. Theological roots were almost always planted in a denominational base, while today's approach is "inter-faith," "multi-faith," "ecumenical." These changes constitute the "yes" answer.

WHAT DO THESE TRENDS SUGGEST RELATIVE TO THE OWNERSHIP OF PASTORAL CARE?

Although professional organizations insist on ties with faith groups as essential for certification, the past 30-40 years have witnessed a diminished interest on the part of judicatories in the actual ministries performed *in situ.* The absence of clear theological contexts for pastoral care is seen by some as problematic. A forthcoming issue of *Christian Bioethics* will focus on the issues of a "generic chaplaincy." It will address questions such as: How do we understand illness theologically? What are the resources of faith vis à vis the "brokenness of life"? Programs that see themselves as "non-denominational" or "inter-faith" or "multi-faith" should, minimally, delineate what biases or beliefs they bring to pastoral care relative to such questions.

Several of the organizations presented herein do address this concern. The Cleveland program explicitly identifies the context from which their pastoral care arises as well as its goals. They even hint at an understanding of theodicy: "Being empowered by the Gospel, the mission . . . is to bring the promise of hope, healing, wholeness and balance to persons experiencing the blessings and brokenness of human life."

The Marketplace Ministries clearly envisions itself as a Christian ministry whose mission includes providing businesses with a "pro-active, personalized faith-based" pastoral care service. While not discussed here, all affiliated chaplains must sign a statement of doctrinal beliefs established by their board.

One might assume a similar heritage for The McFarland Institute in New Orleans. It is operated by Christian Health Ministries which clearly suggests a theological particularity.

The Foundation for Interfaith Research and Ministry provides direct pastoral care "as a congregational activity" based upon three inter-related theological strands: Baptism, Gifts of Spirit, and the New Testament concept of interdependence–i.e., bear one another's burdens. Each of these is more fully described within the article.

The HealthCare Chaplaincy in New York, in contrast, uses the two phrases "not-for-profit" and "health-related" as descriptive of its pastoral care.

Loss of the locus of ministry within Faith groups also raises problems when it comes to funding. Institutions want a pastoral care that its "customers" experience as positive. However, pleasing the recipients of one's ministry may be vastly different from pleasing the sponsors of that ministry, especially when the parameters of that ministry are so minimally defined!

WHAT DO THESE TRENDS SUGGEST RELATIVE TO THE FUNCTIONS OR PRODUCT OF PASTORAL CARE?

The Foundation for Interfaith Research and Ministry is most explicit. Pastoral care is a ministry obligated by one's Baptism; strengthened incarnationally by the Holy Spirit, and requires the "provider" to bear the burdens of the recipients! Further, its ownership is linked to congregations and its providers must include laity [since Baptism demands it of all]. This certainly moves the function of pastoral care away from secular institutions of healing and broadens the product to include development of communities of faith!

The Lutheran program, The McFarland Institute, and Marketplace Ministries also present glimpses of the functions they envision for pastoral care, although less explicitly. Yet the majority suggest that "comfort" and "care" are the functions or products of pastoral care.

Tillich and others suggest that "care" is a universal function between persons. "Comfort" is even less clear, as is true for "help" (i.e., "We 'help' people."). If pastoral care has degenerated to such non-specificity, what really does the chaplain uniquely bring?

"Health-related?" What does that mean? Are chaplains present for "health"? Is pastoral care mainly palliative [i.e., comfort] or is it potentially curative [i.e., Dossey et al.]? Or is it a ministry related to a larger issue such as that suggested by the Foundation for Interfaith Research and Ministry [i.e., the building of the community of faith].

What of the prophetic aspect of pastoral care? Years ago Tony Campolo told a College of Chaplains audience how difficult it was to be a prophet while drawing a salary. These are times when major philosophical issues relative to the care of the sick are being considered. How should sick care be funded? Is sick care a right? What is health? How are we to utilize the resources of allopathic (Western) medicine and homeopathic, napropathic, herbalism, acupuncture, etc.?

Perhaps the very vagueness contributes to the growing trend to placing pastoral care outside organized religion. Spirituality is an example of such vagueness that the major writers today are from fields other than theology. And journals for nurses suggest that they can meet these needs of patients, even to the point of calling the provision "pastoral care."

WHAT DO THESE TRENDS SUGGEST RELATIVE TO THE PROVIDERS OF PASTORAL CARE?

All of these organizations continue in the trend towards equating "quality pastoral care" with "education" and "certification," albeit with a few exceptions. Relative to employment of persons to begin a pastoral care agency, the author of the Lutheran story writes, "Interestingly I do not believe that the person necessarily needs four units of CPE and chaplaincy experience." The Marketplace Ministry program employs a variety of clergy and has primarily a week of orientation. Several others utilize laity in significant numbers.

If the products or functions of pastoral care are essentially "comfort" and "care," that is probably not an issue of great concern. All of them do provide levels of supervision that one hopes would protect recipients of comfort and/or care from overzealous individuals. Still, why would someone pay for such products or functions that are so universal? Probably most clinicians in institutions caring for the sick do intend to be comforting and caring!

If, however, pastoral care does have a theological or philosophical basis and construct, then it is a concern for all of the organizations reporting. Some of them heavily rely upon CPE students to provide pastoral care and, in a few, that provision is located at a site away from the supervisor.

The written materials of ACPE and AAPC are very clear as to the provision of care by trainees. Medicine, Law, Nursing and even Social Work are very clear as regards the use of students. Third party payers are very clear when it comes to reimbursing for students. As more pastoral care providing organizations increase reliance on CPE students and on laity, this trend ought to be explored.

The men and women involved in these organizations are demonstrating the necessity to improvise, to push boundaries, to dare new models, and to follow dreams. Someone once said that the seven last words of any organization are: "We never did it that way before."

Yet it is not enough to just improvise, to push boundaries, to dare new models, and follow dreams. Professionally and individually we must engage the meanings, constructs, ideologies and theologies inherent in such improvisations, altered boundaries, new models. Else what looks like a new dream may, in truth, be nothing more than a nightmare!

A View from My Side of the Hill

George R. Robie, DMin

A drop of water lands on the edge of a spiderweb and the entire web quivers. So it is with the models of contract pastoral care and education in this volume. Each one touches the spiderweb called pastoral care and the entire web quivers. Reverberations occur for three reasons. First, the models challenge numerous assumptions, procedures and structures within the worlds of CPE and pastoral care. Second, they utilize new methods for training clergy and laity in the pastoral arts. Third, they introduce new systems for delivering pastoral care and chaplaincy. The founders of these models are creative thinkers who can discern a need, assess it, and respond within a short time. After investigating the strengths and weaknesses of the models, I feel ambivalent. Part of me favors freestanding centers, part of me is against it, and part of me is cautious. Yes, I am ambivalent, but in the final analysis, the strengths and opportunities are greater than the weakness; therefore, we ought to give these models our hearty support. I will tell you why.

MAKING SERVICES AVAILABLE

The models are a breath of fresh air because they cause CPE and chaplaincy to take a good, hard look at themselves. The models invite the public to claim ownership of clinical education that is good for CPE, the public, and the church. These new forms of training and service incorporate gifts and talents of people who have previously not been involved in the process either as students or board members. The models need our support because they bring

---

George R. Robie is affiliated with the Bryan LGH Medical Center, East, Lincoln, NB 68506.

[Haworth co-indexing entry note]: "A View from My Side of the Hill." Robie, George R. Co-published simultaneously in *Journal of Health Care Chaplaincy* (The Haworth Pastoral Press, an imprint of The Haworth Press, Inc.) Vol. 9, No. 1/2, 1999, pp. 109-116; and: *Contract Pastoral Care and Education: The Trend of the Future?* (ed: Larry VandeCreek) The Haworth Pastoral Press, an imprint of The Haworth Press, Inc., 1999, pp. 109-116. Single or multiple copies of this article are available for a fee from The Haworth Document Delivery Service [1-800-342-9678, 9:00 a.m. - 5:00 p.m. (EST). E-mail address: getinfo@haworthpressinc.com].

difficult issues to the surface by identifying assumptions long taken for granted, turning them around, and re-articulating them in the form of questions. Why can't a supervisor and student be in different geographic locations at the same time during CPE? Why can't chaplaincy be provided as efficiently and at less expense through programs such as "rent a chaplain"? Why can't CPE be entrepreneurial and service oriented at the same time? If it can, what is gained and what is lost? Isn't it possible to organize satellite CPE centers beyond geographical boundaries of a particular region? Are telecommunications, i.e., the internet, videos, and interactive educational television, ideal mediums for CPE? If media is utilized, how does CPE insure that "living human documents" remain the central focus? Such inquiries invite the decision-makers to explore the unknown and be proactive in a time of change. The models deserve support for these and other reasons mentioned above.

The new models are worthy of support because they utilize feedback from professionals outside of theological education. Technology is a good example. The models that utilize technology believe that telecommunication is an important tool, but also that it is to be used to facilitate pastoral education rather than become the focus of it. It is good news to know that futurists will continue to focus on the personal needs of others. The new models cause some dilemmas that, I believe, will bring ultimate good to CPE and chaplaincy. For instance, some of the models are strapped for money, making it a high priority but very destructive when strings are attached. I heard about a proposal for a satellite CPE center at which an individual of means agreed to underwrite the training program if, in the admission process, preference was given to clergy of a certain denomination. Ethically speaking, CPE as I have known it would not want to be associated with that kind of exclusivity? Or would it? As the dollars shrink, centers close, and resources are drained from rural America, is it possible a center might sell out its principles to stay afloat? Who knows? Also, the existence of these and other new models helps CPE and chaplaincy realize the need to write position papers on subjects like entrepreneurial ventures, being part of a larger, national corporation, or being in proprietary relationships. Furthermore, managed care is interested in providing outpatient and inpatient spiritual care because research shows it is cost effective. CPE and chaplaincy need to avoid becoming pawns of the health care system, refusing to be buffers between patients and the costs of their care. The models need our support because their creators are consumer advocates who preserve the values, beliefs, and faith that have through the years served as the underpinnings of CPE.

METHODS AND GOALS FOR A NEW MILLENNIUM

I support the models because they are agents of change that capitalize on present interest in spirituality. People want to explore spirituality, understand it, and grow in it. These goals call attention to the need for qualified spiritual care professionals, but they do not necessarily produce more chaplains or bring relief to a graying profession. The new models are one form of hope in this area because they make CPE more accessible by taking it to areas where training has not been available. Granted, the purpose of CPE is to educate and is broader than preparation for chaplaincy, but the question remains, "Where will our future chaplains come from?" Will there be enough to replace those who are retiring? Also, a shortage of CPE supervisors, fewer people going into ministry, and still fewer willing to put themselves through extra training for chaplaincy does not bode well for the future. The new models encourage chaplains and supervisors to think about these concerns for the future.

The models challenge us to make a leap of faith and give new methodologies a chance. The "we've never done it this way" folks have potential to cripple new initiatives. The naysayers need to lighten up and give permission for experimentation because the future of chaplaincy is at stake. The CPE movement and pastoral care must face up to change. Perhaps we should offer a fast track to chaplaincy and welcome all comers. The nursing profession pioneered the development of fast tracks so if they can do it, why not us? But how shall we maintain quality? Many people are interested in exploring pastoral ministry as a career but have to work full time to maintain a family. Can we accommodate them? When people live a long way from seminary, one finds ways to bring the seminary to them. Bethel Theological Seminary in Minnesota and Bangor Theological Seminary in Maine are doing just that through computer generated distance learning. When persons are located a long way from a CPE center, we need to find ways to bring CPE to them. These kinds of accommodations cause fear that chaplaincy will be watered down, theologically compromised and lose something special if it is one hundred per cent inquirer friendly. On the other hand, movement away from a private, closed system to one with open doors is welcome. A shift from parochial to broad-based interdisciplinary boards is appreciated. When more people sit on a board or are active in the program, there is greater ownership. The models in this volume, by and large, try to maintain quality, establish accountability, and monitor effectiveness. Some do a better job than others. All of them are tenacious in their commitment to training.

In the on-line, e-mail world where undergraduate and graduate degrees are offered by computer, one line CPE and video training in pastoral care can not be far behind. The models in question are part of a larger movement that is growing and will continue to grow. As mentioned above, the trend is driven by change and fed by technological advancements that impact health care at such a pace that ethics, values, and structures have to play catch up. Yet, the new models are doing their best to do so. They are moral and ethical responses to immediate need. They insure pastoral care will be available to populations that might otherwise fall through the cracks. The new models are practical in that they emphasize how an organization should not spend its energy and resources doing what they, the freestanding centers, can do better and for less costs. It is time to welcome these new initiatives because if CPE and chaplaincy put off until tomorrow what can be done today, before anyone knows it, we will be holding a bag of empty yesterdays.

APC and ACPE can do a lot to encourage new ventures. Each issue of *Chaplaincy Today* and *The Journal of Pastoral Care* can showcase new models. The *APC News* can carry requests for skill sharing by persons developing new programs. Those who have "been there" have expertise to lend. The APC annual convention can set aside time to recognize new models and their effectiveness can be discussed at break out sessions. Furthermore, chaplains, supervisors, and CPE ought to encourage trendsetters in pastoral care to combine forces with trendsetters in graduate theological education to design an M.Div. program (including four units of CPE) with an emphasis on pastoral care/chaplaincy. By doing so, CPE can claim a place within academia and students will receive graduate credit while preparing for a career in pastoral ministry. Also, chaplains and pastoral educators need to spend more time interfacing with other disciples because in a time of shifting paradigms, those who will have the greatest impact on the delivery of pastoral care are creative thinkers located outside the box. I am reminded how the National Institute for Healthcare Research spends significant time, energy, and money researching alternative forms of healing. Here is a case where the medical establishment is willing to acknowledge contributions to health care from people outside the mainstream. Why not have a COMISS sponsored team whose sole responsibility is to examine new models, and make recommendations for their applications. These and other methodologies were sparked by the initiative of those who founded the new models. For that reason, the models deserve our support.

BELIEVING, DECIDING, ACTING

If new models are so important, why aren't there more of them? One answer is "enough people don't believe." It was fairly common for a person to approach Jesus and say, "I want to see a miracle, then I will believe." Life does not work that way; first one has to believe and then maybe one can see the miracle. The new models deserve our support because they challenge us to believe and help us see miracles. In new model development, believing takes a huge amount of time, energy, and commitment; in short, it is a labor of love. Believing may mean the founder of the model will be criticized for taking an unpopular stand or going against the mainstream. Consider how easy it is to avoid a fight rather than engage in conflict because, after all, one's career might be on the line. As a result the model is placed on the shelf and forgotten. Creativity may lie dormant because of fears about losing the security and finances that have sustained self and family. It takes an exceptional person to move from the present into the unknown. The models featured in this volume are constantly involved in fund-raising. Some chaplains do not care to be associated with that emphasis.

More models may not be emerging because of the motto of our time: "Do more with less." Where do hard-pressed, hassled, busy people find time to do more? The models found in this volume required significant time, energy, and commitment to get off the ground. A lot of people do not have the time or some have the time but are unwilling to pursue the goal because of uncertainty. Also, as a result of reading this book, it is clear that one needs business savvy in order to develop a new model. Interdisciplinary boards of directors are needed, containing members with a variety of skills such as fund-raising, marketing, knowledge of personnel matters, financial management, grant writing, knowledge of federal employment law and human relations. The ability to create an interdisciplinary board depends on having contacts and influence with decision-makers in the community. There is work to be done and it needs to be done by movers and shakers.

An accredited training center will, of necessity, owe its life to contracts with clinical sites. If some hospitals have pulled the plug on CPE and their own chaplains, they can just as easily pull the plug on contacts with freestanding centers. So, the shift from "deep pocket" institutional funding to community-based funding may also be cause for some to be reluctant participants. You have to believe. To believe is to be committed to the concept and demonstrate a willingness to draw-up the plan and follow through to a conclusion. To believe means to surround yourself with committed people who also believe. Then you may see the miracle. That is, if you have any energy, sanity, or family life left.

The last sentence above indicates I personally do not welcome the opportunity to create a new model for training and education. I am a caregiver rather than a creator of institutions, an introvert who does not have the interest, skill or personality for that kind of work. Furthermore, I am at a place in my career where I want to use my abilities to pursue other goals. The chaplain who creates a new organization must possess a complex mix of organizational ability, people skills, knowledge of organizations, and personnel matters, an understanding of fund-raising, a vision for the future, and personal charisma, as well as an excellent reputation within the community. He or she must be a hard worker and a person of impeccable ethics while being able to articulate the value of the program and move at ease within management and executive circles.

Would I work for a freestanding center? If I had the choice of being a chaplain in a new venture or leaving the profession, I would take a leap of faith and go with the new venture, making sure to obtain as much information as possible ahead of time. I would make sure the venture has broad ecumenical, financial, and community support. I would examine employee satisfaction, other employees' longevity within the company, and how many institutions and individuals are supporting the center with their finances. I would also want to know the value that the center places on certification and where my immediate supervisor fits in the management grid. The models in this volume rise out of the commitment, energy, and management skills of the believers who created them. The models continue to exit because they call on others to believe, decide and act. For this and other reasons mentioned above, they deserve our support.

YOU DECIDE

I believe the preference of most chaplains and CPE supervisors, including myself, is to work for established health care institutions. Why? Because, at least from my viewpoint, they represent stability and presence in the community. Also, the mission and values of established health care institutions may more adequately represent the kind of values that prompted a person to go into chaplaincy in the first place. As a result, there is possibly a closer relationship between institutional and individual goals. The programs of well-established institutions tend to reflect a track record and deeper pockets that can add up to increased job security. The downside is mergemania that turns all institutions into targets for acquisition. What kind of job security is there if the acquirer is not committed to caring for the whole person?

The chaplain who works for a freestanding center has to be a risk taker, one who is excited about reaching out to new clientele. Freestanding centers are intentional about addressing the stresses associated with chaplaincy, giving one the feeling that he or she is cared about in a special way rather than being "another employee with personal issues." Whether the chaplain who works for a freestanding center is more or less financially secure has to be answered on a case-by-case basis. Freestanding centers seem to make it possible for a chaplain to retain affiliation with his or her denomination's pension fund and make clergy housing allowances part of the compensation package. Both are pluses.

Freestanding centers, it seems to me, are probably more open to innovative approaches not only in terms of program but also wage and benefit packages. Established institutions usually have a history of some form of involvement with pastoral services. There may be "in-house" and "community support networks" in place that can be helpful to the chaplain but also detrimental because they can be carriers of unrealistic expectations. Within well-established institutions one finds departments to assist you and ease your way into the marketplace. On the other hand, established institutions may contain a power structure that is hard to work with and says, "there is only one way of doing things here." In addition, one needs to consider the nature of the work chaplains do. Every day chaplains journey into the unknown facing death and losses among patients. We also deal with a constant turnover in nursing and other professionals. In order to function at the optimum, we need anchors such as faith, home, loving relationships, and institutional stability. Personally, I would be less comfortable working in a freestanding center than a well-established institution.

Contract pastoral care and satellite CPE are creative responses to some of the changes occurring in health care. Managed care, downsizing, outsourcing, and elimination of health care services in rural America provide stimulus for the ingenuity behind the centers. Freestanding centers are reaching out and will continue to reach out to congregations and other institutions like extended care facilities, day hospitals, senior day care and clinics. By affiliating with a freestanding center, existing programs will be able to reach more people in depth, in a shorter time because students on clinical assignment will be part of the team and will help institutions fulfill their mission. Some centers will be located in churches and their presence will help strengthen the congregation's outreach to its youth, elderly, and disabled as well as people from the community. Freestanding centers will join forces with parish nurse programs resulting in teams consisting of a parish nurse, lay volunteers, parish visitor and chaplain. Each team can be assigned to a neighborhood.

The new models propose more interfacing between pastors and chaplains. Indeed, the CPE supervisor or chaplain may become a full-time or adjunct staff member of a church causing denominations and congregations to evaluate their approaches to pastoral ministry. Likewise, organizations like the Association of Professional Chaplains and the National Association of Catholic Chaplains will be asked to open their ranks to parish-based chaplains. Congregations may be in competition with new models in areas like recruitment of volunteers or fund-raising. Freestanding centers and their programs of local outreach will be a visible, high-impact type of ministry, forms of local mission, and they may have potential to attract a larger piece of the church's mission dollar. Since many freestanding programs pride themselves in reaching out to a wide variety of ethnic, cultural and faith traditions, they are able to facilitate appreciation for persons of diverse backgrounds. All this contributes to a broader sense of ownership, stewardship and commitment.

Freestanding centers are a viable option for providing training and pastoral care services in a time of shifting values and resources. To say they are "the best answer" or "the answer" is an overstatement. They are "one answer." They represent a smorgasbord of opportunity, and as other models develop, they too will be added to the menu. These new models are being created as a response to requests for education and service, but they are also the result of failure. I am referring to the failure of CPE, pastoral care and chaplaincy to be assertive, visible, and vocal advocates for ourselves on local, state, and national levels. We have a history of not talking about the importance of our work. Not getting the word out has cost us. Positions have been cut, departments eliminated, and some hospitals have gone out of the pastoral care business.

They new models featured in this volume are market oriented. They lift up the value and benefit of the work we do. They are one way of saying, "We will not lose sight of the whole person as a child of God and the need to reach him or her in the most effective way." For all these reasons, the new models deserve our support.

Index

Page numbers followed by fig. indicate figures.

